A Treasury of Cocktail Humor

D1384100

Edited by
James E. Myers

THE LINCOLN-HERNDON PRESS, INC.
818 South Dirksen Parkway
Springfield, Illinois 62703

A Treasury of Cocktail Humor

Published by

Lincoln-Herndon Press, Inc.
818 S. Dirksen Parkway
Springfield, Illinois 62703
(217) 522-2732

Printed in the United States of America

LIBRARY OF CONGRESS CATALOGUING-IN-PUBLICATION DATA

ISBN 0-942936 $10.95
Library of Congress Catalogue Card Number 95-080051
First Printing

Typography by

Communication Design
Rochester, Illinois

Introduction

As a whole, the American people have always enjoyed an occasional — if not often — drink of liquor. Together with this particular pleasure has been the fun in hearing and telling stories and jokes about their fellow drinkers. This combination, liquor and stories, has produced an astonishing reservoir of hilarious tales dealing with drinking booze, hooch, giggle soup, or whatever you wish to call it — and there are more than 600 synonyms for liquor and drunkenness/intoxication.

But together with the fun of drinkers, there has been a vocal, dedicated group of Americans who despise liquor and pity those who drink it. Still, the Bible has many references to the pleasure of drinking — over a hundred of them — and here are three examples of the biblical approval of moderate drinking, from *Cruden's Complete Concordance*. Here wine is used as a cover word for alcoholic beverages.

> "Drink no longer water, but use a little wine for thy stomach's sake and thine often infirmities."
>
> Ecclesiastes. 39:29

> Wine is good as life to a man, if it be drunk moderately. What life is then to a man that is without wine? For it was made to make men glad.
>
> Aprocrypha: 25

> Use a little wine for thy stomach's sake.
>
> Timothy. 5:23

The above references tell us that the euphemism, wine, is a hopeful, biblically endorsed good ... but not to be taken to excess.

This hopeful view of drinking alcoholic beverages is not and was not held by all Americans. Early on, we had a strong, vocal body of Americans who successfully opposed the sale and consumption of alcoholic beverages, and this group took over the nation in 1918 with passage of the Volstead Act. This act led to the 18th Amendment to the Constitution. The sale of alcoholic beverages was prohibited from January 16, 1920 until the law was rescinded by the 21st Amendment to the Constitution on December 5, 1933.

The national prohibition was by no means the first effort to outlaw alcoholic beverages. Many states, in fact 33 of them, had their own laws prohibiting the sale of "booze." The battle against such sales was led by the Anti-Saloon League, a national and very militant group with tremendous power at that time.

It seems clear that the United States has always been a battle ground of those who favor free sale and consumption of liquor and those who don't!

Certainly, both before and after the 1920s, it was proven that you cannot stop Americans from making and drinking "hooch," cocktails, "giggle soup," much less control their drinking. That earlier time and those laws brought America some of the worst crime, murder, theft, that the nation has ever seen. Today, we do have excessive drinking, but we have discovered other, more peaceful and effective ways to handle it, such as Alcoholics Anonymous, licenses, education, etc. But the use of alcoholic beverages is and always will be a problem that is lessened by use of all the superb humor that has evolved out of the struggle.

The following jokes, stories, cartoons represent the best humor that has evolved out of this major American amusement, escape, therapy, etc. The jokes, stories, cartoons offer a universe of fun for both drinkers and non-drinkers and offer insights to the world of both moderate and immoderate drinkers of ... of ... "angel juice." And, the best of them are on the following pages.

If you drink, don't drive. Don't even putt.

Dean Martin

The bell captain at the Hilton Hotel in Chicago got a phone call from a guest at 2 A.M.! "What time does the bar open?" the voice asked.

"It opens at 10 A.M., Sir," and then he hung up.

A half hour later, the same guy calls back and asks the same question. "As I told you, Sir, the bar opens at 10 A.M.!" replied the bell captain.

A little over an hour later, the phone rings again and it is the same guy with the same question: "When does your bar open?"

"I'll tell you once more and then I don't want to hear from you again. There is no way you can get in the bar until ten."

"Get in?" the caller says, "Hell, I don't want to get in the bar, I want to get out!"

"One swallow doesn't make a summer but too many swallows make a fall."

George D. Prentice — 1802-1870

Dr. Ed Reich was good at his profession, but he had this one weakness ... he loved to gamble. So, one evening, done with his practice, he cashes a check for $1,000 and wanders over to his favorite gambling joint. Once inside, he has a double shot of scotch with a beer chaser, then goes to the dice tables and lays out a $500 bet, takes the dice and throws them on the table, but ... a third die rolls out of his sleeve onto the table! The people crowded around the table gasped! The dealer picks up all three dice, puts one of them in his pocket and says, "Now, Doctor, you can roll again. Your point is sixteen."

"All of a sudden it doesn't like water anymore!"

The physician asked his patient, an old man, if he drank liquor.

"About a quart of whiskey a day ... that's all," he replied.

"And smokin' ... you smoke?"

"Yeah ... couple of packs a day."

"Just as I suspected. Now you must do exactly as I tell you, Sir, or you won't live long. You will have to quit drinking and smoking and that means, RIGHT NOW! Got that?"

The old man stood, hitched-up his pants and started out.

"Hey, Sir, I don't run a charity ward. You owe me twenty dollars for my advice!"

"Who's taking it?" the old man said, and left.

"There are two reasons for drinking: One is when you are thirsty, to cure it; the other, when you are thirsty, to prevent it."

Thomas Peacock — 1785-1866

Eddie Stevens was caught in the rain so he turned into a large church where a famous evangelist was conducting services. It was much drier in there, Eddie figured. So, he entered, walked down the aisle and took a seat. Services began soon after and the subject this Sunday was: "Alcohol and Those Who Drink It."

It was an enthralling lecture and Eddie, who rarely attended church, was enthralled. The preacher ended his sermon saying: "Who has the most money in town? We all know. The liquor store owner. And who has the most expensive house in the best neighborhood? Again, we all know who it is ... the liquor store owner. And who dresses his wife in mink coats and jewels and drives a Cadillac? Obviously, it is the liquor store owner. And who makes it possible to have all these expensive things? My friends, you do ... hard working folks like you! That's who! You who spend your money for beer and whiskey and wine!"

At the close of services, Eddie rushed to the pulpit and shook hands with the preacher, saying, "Thanks a million, Reverend Preacher. I'm so grateful to you. You are something else!"

"Then you are saved, my good man?" asked the minister. "You are not going to drink any more?"

"I don't know about that," said Eddie. "But I do know that I'm going right out and buy me a liquor store."

"I am a stylist, and the most beautiful sentence I have ever heard is 'Have One on the House.'"

Wilson Mizner — 1876-1933

He had celebrated a bit too much with his equally old buddies who had attended a Christmas celebration at their favorite bar. Ed Pistorius had had a truly good time and now, nearly 2:00 A.M., he was trying to walk his way home. He had to cross a bridge to get there and half way over it, he stopped to lean on the rail and look down at the water below. For a moment, he was stunned. He simply couldn't believe what he saw. Just imagine!

A policeman saw him swaying back and forth on the railing and ran over to him. "Get away from that rail, old man!" the cop yelled. Ed pulled back, obeying the officer.

"Now, old man, you get on home before I haul you in to jail!" the policeman growled. "Aren't you ashamed of yourself ... an old man like you!"

"Sure, I'll go. But tell me, officer, what's that sh-h-hiny thing, d-d-down there?"

The officer looked down, then said, "That's the moon, the moon. Got that?"

"That's what I thought. But I couldn't believe it," he said, lifting his eyes toward heaven. "Dear God, I sure do thank you. Now I know. Before I wasn't ever sure I'd make it to heaven!"

Never refuse wine. It is an odd but universally held opinion that anyone who doesn't drink must be an alcoholic.

P. J. O'Rourke

He was an old geezer, also a practiced boozer known for his intelligence and learning. Unfortunately, he was caught out one night by the police and now stands before a judge. "You are charged with drunk and disorderly conduct," the judge says. "Do you have anything to say to the court before you are sentenced?"

The old guy gets up, faces the crowd and then the judge. He speaks: "Man's inhumanity to man is the raison d'etre for the mourning of all men." Then the old guy begins to pace and wave his arms as he says, "I, Sir, am not so debased as Shakespeare, nor so corrupt as Poe, nor so mindless as Keats, so cowardly as Tennyson, so mindless in my drinking as Burns, so ..."

With that, the Judge stands up and he is furious. "That'll be enough out of you! And you get ninety days!" The Judge turns to the sheriff: "Sheriff, make a list of all those guys that prisoner quoted and go get every last one of 'em. They're even worse than the defendant!"

"Drinking makes such fools of people, and people are such fools to begin with, that it's compounding a felony."

Robert Benchley

A fellow walks into his favorite bar and he is a mess! His left eye is black and swollen shut! Blood drips from his mouth and his left cheek is black and blue. "Hey, man, who messed you up like that?" the bartender asked.

"I had a fight with Pete McHugh!"

"Pete McHugh? That tiny jerk! You let a little, weak old pussy cat like Pete beat you up?"

"Hold on, man. Don't be so hasty in your judgment and you ought not speak so disrespectfully of the dead!"

"I drink when there is an occasion, and sometimes when there is no occasion."

Miguel D. Cervante — 1547-1616

An old bum who is living on the streets of New York heard that his brother in Chicago was deathly ill. He felt he must be with his brother during these last days of his life, but he has no money. Never mind. He goes to work on the streets of New York and begs enough money to buy his ticket. He goes to the airport, makes it to the ticket counter and puts down his money, all of it! Sadly, the clerk informs him that he's a nickel short of enough to pay for his Chicago ticket.

The bum excuses himself and goes out to the entrance of the airport terminal. He speaks to the first man to come by: "Sir, could you let me have a nickel? I need it to get to Chicago."

The guy looks at the bum and says, "Here's a quarter. Now you take four of your buddies."

———————————

"Absence makes the heart grow fonder."

Addison Mizner — 1872-1933

———————————

Judge Noah S. Sweat, Jr. was a member of the House of Representatives of Mississippi in the early 1950s. He made a speech in 1952 that achieved national fame, and one Mississippi legislator described it as the "most famous oration of this century."

It is a superb example of ironic speech and met the approval of most of his Mississippi contemporaries. It marks a highlight in political irony and humor. His speech addressed an issue paramount in the minds of Americans of two generations ago ... whether to legalize liquor or to continue Prohibition.

My Friends. I had not intended to discuss this controversial subject at this particular time. However, I want you to know that I do not shun controversy. On the contrary, I will take a stand on any issue at any time, regardless of how fraught with controversy it might be. You have asked me how I feel about whiskey. All right, here is how I feel about whiskey ... If when you say whiskey you mean the devil's brew, the poison scourge, the bloody monster that defiles innocence, dethrones reason; destroys the home, creates misery and poverty, yea literally takes the bread from the mouths of little children: if you mean the evil drink that topples the Christian man and woman from the pinnacle of righteous, gracious living into the bottomless pit of degradation and despair, and shame and helplessness and hopelessness, then certainly I am against it.

But ...

If when you say whiskey you mean the oil of conversation, the philosophic wine, the ale that is consumed when good fellows get together that puts a song in their hearts and laughter on their lips, and the warm glow of contentment in their eyes: if you mean Christmas cheer: if you mean the stimulating drink that puts the spring into the old gentleman's step on a frosty, crispy morning: if you mean the drink that enables a man to magnify his joy and his happiness, and to forget, if only for a little while, life's great tragedies, and heartaches and sorrows: if you mean that drink, the sale of which pours into our treasuries untold millions of dollars, which are used to provide tender care for our little crippled children, our blind, our deaf, our dumb, our pitiful aged and infirm: to build highways and hospitals and schools, then certainly I am for it. This is my stand. I will not retreat from it. I will not compromise.

Reprinted with permission. Copyright © 1988 by Noah S. Sweat, Jr. (Parchment. embossed-letter copies of the speech, suitable for framing, are available for $7.95 from Political Classics, Box 2323, Corinth, MS 38834. Signed and numbered copies are $11.95. Add $2 for shipping and handling.)

"Inflation has gone up over a dollar a quart."

W. C. Fields

"Yeah, man, I agree that money talks. It's been saying goodbye to me for years!"

This old drunk was wandering down the street in the old red light district when he saw a naked couple lying unconscious and belly-to-belly, beside the entrance steps. He works his way up the steps, knocks on the door and, just as it opened, says to the madam: "Lady, jusht want to t-tell ya that y-your sign fell d-down."

"Taverns are places where madness is sold by the bottle."

Jonathan Swift — 1667-1745

Did you hear about the sad event that occurred during a showing of an old time circus? Well, it seems that the performing fire-eater had been drinking pints of corn liquor just before he was to perform his act. At the performance, he lit the match for the fire he was to eat and there was an enormous explosion and that poor guy almost burned to death.

"Drink the first. Sip the second slowly. Skip the third."

Knute Rockne

There was a young lady from Berlin,
Who thought that to love was a sin.
But when she was tight
It all seemed quite right,
So everyone filled her with gin.

LIMERICKS — THE POETRY OF FUN-LOVERS

There was an old drunkard of Hebron,
Who died and ascended to Heaven;
But he cried: "This must be Hades —
There are no naughty ladies
And the pubs are all shut by eleven."

At the age of 103, Hermann Smith-Johannsen said, "The secret to a long life is to stay busy, get plenty of exercise and don't drink too much. Then again ... don't drink too little."

I went with the Duchess to tea,
Her manners were shocking to see;
Her rumblings abdominal
Were simply phenomenal,
And everyone thought it was me.

"Men's evil manners live in rum. Their virtues we write in water."

Shakespeare

Not that it always transpired
That it turned out quite as desired;
One gent of Ghent
Was undoubtedly bent,
And he didn't advance — he retired.

"Does he drink? Why, if there's a nip in the air he'll have a try at it."

There was a young lady of Trent,
Who said that she knew what it meant
When men asked her to dine
With cocktails and wine,
She knew what it meant — but she went.

A condemned man was brought from his cell blindfolded and made to stand ready for execution. "You are entitled to a last wish that we will grant before you die," said the guard.

"My only request is to be allowed to sing my favorite song all the way through with no interruptions," the condemned man replied.

The officer said: "Your wish is granted. You may begin to sing."

The prisoner then began:

"Twenty million bottles of beer on the wall,
Twenty million bottles of beer.
If one of those bottles should happen to fall,
Nineteen million, 999 bottles of beer on the wall.
Nineteen million, 999 bottles of beer ..."

"Reminds me of my safari in Africa. Somebody forgot the corkscrew and for several days we had to live on nothing but food and water."

W. C. Fields

"Mary, darling, I got to tell you that for the first time in weeks, I slept like a log last night."
"You must have because I found you in the fireplace this morning!"

Ever since Paul Brown got back from his tour of duty in Iraq, he's suffered from "bottle fatigue!"

There was this perpetual drunk who simply couldn't quit boozing. But now the guy claims he hasn't touched a drop ... since they invented the funnel.

Emil likes to boast to company that he hasn't had a hangover in ten years. But his wife always corrects him by saying: "Of course not. That's because you haven't been sober in ten years!"

Then there was the musician who decided to write a new beer-drinking song. But he ran into too much trouble and couldn't get past the first two bars!

You are not an alcoholic if you drink nothing stronger than gin before breakfast.

W. C. Fields

W. C. Fields always took a huge cocktail shaker with him wherever he went to perform. He told people it was filled with pineapple juice. One day an attendant in the theatre actually poured the thing full of pineapple juice and Fields, when he took his regular drink from it, yelled, "Somebody has been putting pineapple juice in my pineapple juice!"

W. C. Fields was introduced to brandied figs by a friend. After eating several of them, Fields declared: "I never ate so much to drink in my life!"

There is a guy in Decatur, Illinois, who was so drunk that on his seventieth birthday, he lit all the candles on his own birthday cake with one breath!

"Hey there mishter Doorman, call me a cab."
"What? You've got a nerve, Mister. I'm no doorman ... I'm an admiral!"
"Ya don't shay! So call me a boat!"

Robert Benchley to his valet: "Let's get out of these wet clothes and into a dry martini!"

Concerning the dry martini, James Thurber said, "One is all right, two is too many, three is not enough!"

The famous early American Henry Clay once said, "What makes this country strong is the two-party system ... party on Friday night and another on Saturday."
"The worst thing about some men is that when they aren't drunk, they're sober."
William Butler Yeats — 1865

A passerby was stopped by a bum who asked him for a dollar to get something to eat. The passerby told the bum that he did not give money to beggars but that he would buy him a drink. "No thanks," said the bum. "I don't drink."

"Well, then, let me give you a cigarette."

"Thanks, but no. I don't smoke," said the bum.

The passerby said, "I'm trying to help you but I simply don't give money. Got that? One thing more I'll do. I'm going to place a bet on my favorite horse. I was on my way when you stopped me. To help you, I'll put two bucks on that horse for you. OK?"

"No sir, please don't. I don't gamble. I need only a buck to get a bite to eat. That's all."

Finally, the passerby gave in. "OK," he said, "I'll go with you to the restaurant and buy you a good dinner. But after that, you must go with me to my home, OK?"

The bum agreed. So, after he had his free dinner, the bum joined his benefactor on the trip to the latter's home. When his wife opened the door, the man said, "Honey, I want you to take a good, hard look at this bum. I just want you to see what happens to a man who doesn't drink or smoke or gamble!"

The famous old-time actor, John Barrymore, loved martinis. He went to a bar one evening and asked for a dry martini ... "twenty parts gin to one part vermouth."

"Shall I put a slice of lemon peel in it, Sir?" asked the bartender.

"No! When I want a lemonade, I'll ask for it," Barrymore replied.

"As far as I know Mr. Goodyear isn't hosting a black tire affair."

"I recently read a book on the evils of drinking, so I quit reading."

A fellow once remarked that he loved the good life of wine, women and song. His buddy asked, "Tell me ... since I know that song is not so important to you, but if you had to make a choice between wine or women ... which would you choose?"

The guy seemed lost in study, then said, "My choice in both cases would depend on the vintage."

There was a fellow in Los Angeles who got so heavily loaded with booze that they made him take the freight elevator.

The poor girl had been married only three months when her mother dropped by the home and found her daughter in tears. "Dear, what is the matter?" her mother asked.

"It's him, my husband! Oh, I'm so upset. He's drunk all the time, morning, noon and night."

"Oh my goodness!" exploded the mother. "If you knew that, why did you marry him?"

"I didn't know he drank," the girl sobbed, "until he came home one night ... sober!"

Water taken in moderation cannot hurt anybody.

Mark Twain

The guy had one terrific hangover, a truly giant-sizer! "Susie," he groaned to his wife, "get me the aspirin in the bathroom, please." She left as quietly as possible, tip-toeing out. She came back with a tin of aspirin, handed him a pill that he took at once, saying, "Now please, fer-gaw'd sake, don't slam the lid!"

Don't try to drown your sorrows. They are the best swimmers in the world.

Elmer Toddler was really mad at the police officer who had arrested him for being intoxicated. And in court he told the judge just that. "Judge, I' shust as shober ash you are. I ain't drunk ... one ... bit."

"Officer, tell the court what made you think the defendant was drunk."

"First, let me tell it like it wash, Judge. I was shust kneelin' in the hh-h-highway, on my handsh and knees. That's all. When thish geek arreshted me."

"Your honor," said the officer involved, "he was trying to roll up that little white line in the middle!"

"I happen to think that the three-martini lunch is the epitome of American efficiency.

Where else can you get an earful, a bellyful and a snootful at the same time?"

Gerald Ford — 38th U.S. President

Eddie Blake was plumb stinko. They said his blood registered 90 proof! He staggered into the saloon, struggled his way to the bar, slid onto a stool and said to the guy sitting next to him: "Hey, buddy, I ain't Sunday and I ain't Monday or Tuesday or even Wednesday. So do you know who I am?"

"Are you Thursday?"

"Am I! Bartender, this guy just offered to buy me a drink!"

Here are five simple tests to determine the individual's sobriety: Three are verbal and two are visual; taken one after another, you can't go wrong on any of 'em.

These five tests were actually devised in 1937 and published in a book of factual integrity: *The Drunk's Blue Book.*

Test No.1 The Glass Arm. This test is a very simple one and may be tried out in any public building which dispenses spirituous beverages. See how near to the edge of a table you can place a full highball glass without its falling off. If you miss the table entirely you are slightly inebriated. If there is no glass in your hand when you do the trick, you are just plain cockeyed but if there's no glass in your hand and no table in sight, brother, you're fried!

Test No. 2. The Girder-Upper. Select a skyscraper under construction and ascend to the fourth or fifth floor. Pick out a long naked girder and walk (do not run) along it. If you reach the other side you are perfectly sober, but if you lie down and go to sleep, thinking you are in your own apartment, you're mildly soused. And if you start hunting around for the janitor to complain about the heat, you're only a step from a drunkard's grave.

Drunkenness Test No. 3. Find a policeman, one preferably six feet tall and weighing in the neighborhood of two hundred pounds. (The tougher the neighborhood the better.) If you can stand on his shoulders for ten minutes without knocking off his hat you're as sober as a judge. Soberer.

Here is a visual test, quite simple, to determine your sobriety or the reverse. Brave souls can add a chair or two while timid folks can use only three or four. Conclusions can vary depending on the choices made.

The materials needed for this fool-proof test are simple and startlingly available. Simply explore your basement, attic, or most seldom-used closets and you'll find them.

Another test for sobriety!

Reprinted from *Drunk's Blue Book*
by Norman Anthony and O. Soglow.
New York: Frederick A. Stoke Co., 1933.

I drink every known alcoholic drink and enjoy 'em all. I learned early in life how to handle alcohol and never had any trouble with it. The rules are simple as mud: first, never drink if you've got any work to do. Never. If I've got a job of work to do at ten o'clock at night I won't take a drink until that time. Secondly, never drink alone. That's the way to become a drunkard. And thirdly, even if you haven't got any work to do, never drink while the sun is shining. Wait until it's dark. By that time you're near enough to bed to recover quickly.

H. L. Mencken

A man is a fool if he drinks before he reaches fifty, and a fool if he doesn't drink afterward.

Frank Lloyd Wright

———

A dipsy drunk was boarding the subway in New York City and the crowd was awful. He worried a bit about the bottle on his hip, what with all the pushing and shoving, but just standing erect so occupied his mind that he forgot about his bottle of angel fluid. He was standing amidst all the turmoil when the fellow beside him said, "Hey, Buddy, there's some kind of liquid trickling down your leg onto the floor."

"O my gawd!" gasped the drunk, "I hope it's blood!"

———

Getting soused to cure your worries is like cleaning a gas tank with a blow torch ... the results are a lot more certain than your chance to enjoy them.

———

A drunk, wandering down the street, was suddenly hit with an overpowering need to go to the bathroom. He saw a church and walked up its steps to enter the sanctuary. He wandered about, finally sitting down in the confessional. A priest was busy with confession on the other side. Finished with that confession, the priest closed the window and opened the one on the side where the drunk was seated. Trying to get the drunk's attention, he knocked on the window only to be told, "ain't no use knockin', there ain't no paper over here either."

———

"One more drink and I'll be under the host."

Dorothy Parker

If all be true that I do think,
There are five reasons why we should drink:
Good wine — a friend — or being dry —
Or lest we should be by and by —
Or any other reason why.

Dr. Henry Aldrich

Two drunks were staggering down the railroad tracks when one muttered, "I never shaw so many damned steps in my life."

The other one groaned between burps: "It ain't the shteps th-that's abotherin' me, itsh these low r-railings!"

"An alcoholic is someone you don't like who drinks as much as you."

Dylan Thomas

A farmer had been to town Saturday night and had taken on a huge load of giggle soup. He managed to make it back home, pulled up to the gate, stopped his pickup, unlocked and opened the gate, drove his truck through, then stopped and got out of the truck. He closed the gate, leaving enough space to step through, did step through and pulled the gate shut, leaving him standing on the outside. He turned around and walked toward the house, couldn't find it, lay down for a nap and slept till morning.

He was one embarrassed farmer when he realized what he'd done!

First you take a drink, then the drink takes a drink, then the drink takes you.

F. Scott Fitzgerald

BALLAD OF A YOUNG MAN
As sung by Helen Ramsey

There was a young man, and he came to New York, to find him-self a lu-cra-tive po-si-tion be-fit-ting his tal-ents. And he haunt-ed all the Em-ploy-ment A-gen-cies, but was near-ly starved to death, When at last he got a job in a stone quar-ry with all the oth-er Col-lege grad - - u - ates.

And after Work was done
they lured him into a Saloon
and tempted him to drink
a glass of Beer.

But he'd promised his dear old Mother
that he never would Imbibe,
that he'd never touch his Lips to a glass
containing Liquor.

They laughed at him and Jeered
and they called him a cow-yard
Till at last he clutched and drained
the glass of Beer.

When he seen what he had Did
he dashed his glass upon the floor
and Staggered out the door
with Delirium Tremens.

And the first person that he met
was a Salvation Army Lass
and with one kick he broke
her Tambourine.

When she seen what he had Did
She placed a Mark upon his Brow
with a kick that she had learned before
she was Saved.

And the Moral of this tale
is to Shun that Fatal glass
and don't go around kicking
Other people's Tambourines.

More Pious Friends and Drunken Companions
by Frank Shay.
The Macauley Company

For a bad hangover, take the juice of two quarts of whiskey.

Eddie Condon

FLOWERY LANGUAGE

"Aloe, Vera."
"Hyacinth."
"Iris wondering how yew were."
"It aspen a long time."
"Thistle be a fine party. Is little Primrose coming?"
"Promise not to tell this?"
"Oak-ay. Mum's the word."
"Acorn-ing to the gravevine, Gladiolus gets drunk."
"That's really yucca! She'd butternut do that here. It's cheshnut right."

"Wood you believe she used to be a tree-totaler?"
"That's a-maize-ing. Did Cyclamen come with you?"

Pun-American Newsletter by
Charlotte Hatfield, Rock Island, Ill.

"A man is never drunk if he can lay on the floor without holding on."

Joe E. Lewis

An old guy in southern Mississippi thought that he was dying. As evening approached, he called to his wife and she came and stood bedside.

"Honey," he whispered, "you know that old trunk in the basement?"

"Yes dear, ... I do," she replied tearfully.

"Go fetch it and take out of it a bottle of real old bourbon that's in it, will ya?"

"Sure, dear, I'll do it. At once. But then what?"

"You open it in the kitchen, pour a glass half full, fill it with ice, put a bit of mint in it. And then you bring it to me. And then, no matter what I say or do ... you make me take it!"

It only takes one drink to get me loaded. The trouble is, I can't remember if it's the thirteenth or the fourteenth.

A famous scientist, known for his powers of reasoning and for his nasty disposition, was drinking with his students on New Year's Eve. They thought it a good time to get even with their instructor for all the work he had made them do. So when the professor was quite drunk they hauled him out to the cemetery where they laid him at the head of a tombstone, covered him with blankets and left him there.

When he awakened in the morning, he looked around, scratched his head in bewilderment, then said, "If I'm living, what am I doing in a cemetery? And if I'm dead, why do I have to urinate!"

Brandy and water spoils two good things.

Charles Lamb

LIMERICKS! AH, LIMERICKS

A bibulous chap from Duquesne,
Drank a whole jeroboam of champagne.
Said he with a laugh,
As he quaffed the last quaff,
I tried to get drunk but in vuesne.

At a bistro, a chap named O'Reilly,
Said, "I've heard these martinis praised heilly,
But they're better by far
At the neighboring bar
Where they're mixed much more smoothly and dreilly."

BIBLE STORIES

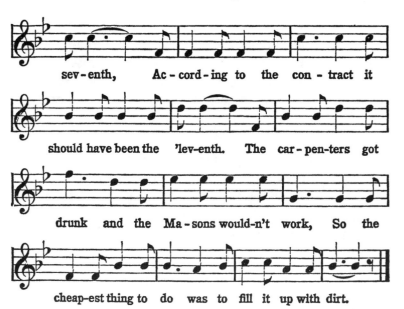

The earth was made in six days and fin-ished on the sev-enth, Ac-cord-ing to the con-tract it should have been the 'lev-enth. The car-pen-ters got drunk and the Ma-sons would-n't work, So the cheap-est thing to do was to fill it up with dirt.

Chorus

Old folks, young folks, everybody come,
Join our little Sunday school and make yourselves at
    home.
Kindly check your chewing gum and razors at the
    door,
And we'll tell you Bible stories that you never heard
    before.

Adam was the first man and Eve she was his spouse;
They lost their job for stealing fruit and went to
    keeping house.
All was very peaceful and quiet on the main
Until a little baby came and they started raising Cain.

Chorus

The Lord made the devil, and the devil made sin;
The Lord made a cubbyhole to put the devil in.
The devil got sore and said he wouldn't stay;
The Lord said he had to, 'cause he couldn't get away.

Chorus

Cain he raised potatoes and he peddled them in town.
Abel called him hayseed every time he came around
Cain he laid a stick of wood on brother Abel's head,
And when he took that stick away, he found poor Abel
    dead.

Chorus

Noah was the keeper of the Asiatic zoo;
He built an ocean liner when he hadn't much to do;
One day he got excited when the sky was getting
    dark,
So he gathered all his animals and put them in the
    ark.

Chorus

It rained for forty days and it rained for forty nights,
The water washed the land completely out of sight!
But when Noah was a-wondering as to what he'd
    better do,
The ark hit Mount Ararat and stuck as tight as glue!

Chorus

Methuselah is famous, because he couldn't croak,
Although he finally grew to be an old and seedy bloke.
He had so many whiskers that you couldn't see his
    head;
If he'd lived a little longer, he'd have used them for his
    bed.

Chorus

Elijah was an aeronaut, or else I am a liar,
He ascended up to heaven in a chariot of fire;

His eccentric disappearance gave the Israelites a
   shock,
They said he beat the Wright brothers by fully half a
   block.

Chorus

Abraham was a patriarch, the father of his set;
He took his little Ikey out to kill him on a bet.
And he'd have met his finish if it wasn't for a lamb,
For papa had his razor out and didn't give a damn!

Chorus

Esau was a cowboy of a wild and woolly make,
His father gave him half the land and half to brother
   Jake;
But when he saw his title to the land it wasn't clear —
He sold it to his brother for a sandwich and a glass of
   beer!

Chorus

Daniel was a brave man who wouldn't mind the king;
The king he said he never heard of such a thing;
Thrust him down a man-hole with lions all beneath,
But Daniel was a dentist — and pulled the lion's teeth!

Chorus

Jonah was an emigrant, so runs the Bible tale,
He took an ocean voyage in a transatlantic whale.
The whale was over-crowded which put Jonah to
   distress,
So Jonah pushed the button and the whale did all the
   rest.

Chorus

David was a shepherd's boy, his mother's pride and
   joy;
His father gave him a slingshot, a harmless little toy.
Along came Goliath, a-looking for a fuss,
David heaved a cobblestone and caved in his crust.

Chorus

Samson was a strong man of the John L. Sullivan
　　school;
He killed a thousand Philistines with the jawbone of a
　　mule!
Along came a woman who filled him up with gin,
And shaved off his whiskers and the coppers pulled
　　him in.

Final Chorus

Walk in, walk in, walk in, I say,
Walk into the parlor and hear the banjos play,
Walk into the parlor and hear the banjos ring,
And see the old boy's finger a-picking on the string.

More Pious Friends and Drunken Companions
by Frank Shay.
The Macauley Company

————————

"A lady temperance candidate concluded her passionate oration: 'I would rather commit adultery than take a glass of beer.' A loud voice from the audience shouted: 'Who wouldn't?'"

Adlai Stevenson

————————

He was really drunk and stumbling through a cemetery when he fell into a grave. A few minutes later along came another drunk, and he fell in, too. After a while, the first drunk looked at the second drunk and said, "Gosh, it's cold in here." And the second drunk said, "Well, no wonder, you kicked all the dirt off you!"

————————

"Sometimes too much to drink is barely enough."

Mark Twain

"All of a sudden it doesn't taste like water anymore!"

"You say my wife is outspoken? By whom?"

TOASTS THAT MIGHT COME IN HANDY

"To marriage: The happy state which resembles a pair of shears; so joined that they cannot be separated; often moving in opposite directions, yet always punishing any one who comes between them."

A toast to Dan Cupid, the great evil-doer,
merciless rogue — may his darts ne'er grow fewer.

Estelle Foreman

"Here's to the prettiest,
Here's to the wittiest,
Here's to the truest of all who are true;
Here's to the neatest one,
Here's to the sweetest one,
Here's to them all in one — here's to you!"

"Here's to God's first thought, 'Man'!
Here's to God's second thought, 'Woman'!
Second thoughts are always best,
So, here's to Woman!"

———

"To woman, the only loved autocrat who elects without
    voting,
Governs without law, and decides without appeal."

———

"We haven't all had the good fortune to be ladies; we
have not all been generals, or poets or statesmen; but
when the toast works down to the babies, we stand on
common ground — for we've all been babies."

Mark Twain

———

Laugh at all things,
Great and small things,
Sick or well, at sea or shore:
While we are quaffing
Let's have laughing
Who the devil cares for more.

Byron

———

Some talk got out about the Justices of the Supreme
Court drinking too much. They all lived at the same
house in Washington. They did not bring their wives to
Washington with them, as the accommodations were
frightful. They boarded together at 2-1/2 Street, called
Marshall Place. That house still stands. They lived
together like a sort of family and discussed their cases
all the time; but they had every Saturday as "consultation
day" at the capital.

There came to be a little talk about the Justices
drinking too much, even then. So (John) Marshall said,
"Now, gentlemen, I think that with your consent I will

make it a rule of this Court that hereafter we will not drink anything on consultation day — that is, except when it rains."

The next consultation day — I think the Court went on the water wagon during the week — when they assembled, Marshall said to Story, "Will you please step to the window and look out and examine this case and see if there is any sign of rain." Story looked out the window, but there was not a sign of rain ... He came back and seriously said to the Chief Justice, who was waiting for the result, "Mr. Chief Justice, I have very carefully examined this case. I have to give it as my opinion that there is not the slightest sign of rain."

Marshall said, "Justice Story, I think that is the shallowest and most illogical opinion I have ever heard you deliver; you forget that our jurisdiction is as broad as this Republic, and by the laws of nature, it must be raining some place in our jurisdiction. Waiter, bring on the rum."

Treasury of American Anecdotes by B. A. Botkin
Galahad Publishers N.Y., 1982

I was in love with a beautiful blonde once. She drove me to drink. Tis the one thing I'm indebted to her for.

W. C. Fields

The following account, entitled "I Had Eighteen Bottles," is supposedly authentic. Even if it isn't, it has made the editors of eighteen joke books very happy:

I had eighteen bottles of whiskey in my cellar and was told by my wife to empty the contents of each and every bottle down the sink, or else ... I said I would and proceeded with the unpleasant task. I withdrew the cork from the first bottle and poured the contents down the sink with the exception of one glass which I drank.

I extracted the cork from the second bottle and did likewise with it with the exception of one glass, which I drank. I then withdrew the cork from the third bottle and poured the whiskey down the sink which I drank.

I pulled the cork from the fourth bottle down the sink and poured the bottle down the glass, which I drank. I pulled the bottle from the cork of the next and drank one sink out of it, and threw the rest down the glass. I pulled the sink out of the next glass and poured the cork down the bottle. Then I corked the sink with the glass, bottled the drink and drank the pour.

When I had everything emptied, I steadied the house with one hand. I counted the glasses, corks, bottles, and sinks with the other which were 29, and as the house came by, I counted them again, and finally had all the houses in one bottle, which I drank.

I'm not under the afluence of incohol, as some tinkle peep I am. I'm not half as thunk as you might drink. I fool so feelish I don't know who is me, and the drunker I stand here the longer I get. Oh me!

TOASTS FOR THE READER

"Here's to the gladness of her gladness when she's
    glad!
Here's to the sadness of her sadness when she's sad!
But the gladness of her gladness
And the sadness of her sadness
Are not in it with her madness when she's mad!"

LINES TO A BOTTLE OF WHISKY KEPT ON A CERTAIN SIDEBOARD FOR "MEDICINAL PURPOSES ONLY"

A plague, a murrain and a pox, say I,
Upon one who, possessing liquid rye,
Hedges it round with rulings that promote

Fictitious coughs from the designing throat!
What of a home where the parched guest must sink
In a feigned stupor to procure a drink;
Where spurious symptoms, carefully rehearsed
Are more effective than an honest thirst?

CHAMPAGNE

Here's to champagne, the drink divine,
That makes us forget our troubles;
It's made of a dollar's worth of wine
And six dollars' worth of bubbles.

Here's to "Block and Tackle" whiskey — take a drink,
walk a block and tackle anything.

TO MARRIAGE

Here's to the wings of love,
May they never moult a feather
Till your little shoes and my big boots
Are under the bed together.

Here's to that most fascinating woman, the widow of
some other man!

Carolus Ager

Here's to the man who loves his wife
And loves his wife alone,
For many a man loves another man's wife
When he ought to be loving his own.

Burns

Here's to love, the only fire against which there is no
insurance.

So let us all; yes, by that love which all our life
  rejoices,
By those dear eyes that speak to us with love's
  seraphic voices,
By those dear arms that will enfold us when we sleep
  forever,
By those dear lips that kiss the lips that may give
  answer never,
By mem'ries lurkin' in our hearts an' all our eyes
  bedimmin',
We'll drink a health to those we love an' who love us
  — the wimmin!

Eugene Field

"The doctor put Otis on a one beer a day diet."

They say there's microbes in a kiss.
This rumor is most rife,
Come lady dear, and make of me an invalid for life.

Two old friends, buddies since grade school and now in their seventies, were together at the last day of one of them. The sick man, Peter, could not live through the night. "I'm about to kick-off, Pat," the dying man said. "Do me one last favor. There's a fine bottle of bourbon in my kitchen and I can't drink it. So I ask that you take it to the cemetery and pour it over my grave. Will you do that for me?"

"Of course, I will! But one thing, would it be OK to run it through my kidneys first?"

When drinking, remember not to squat with your spurs on.

(Cowboy advice)

Here's a tale about the man with the most sensitive tongue in Kentucky.

Long ago, Senator Blackburn and Senator Beck were asked by a friend to go to his room to sample a jug of McBrayer whiskey.

They accepted, went to his room and each took a drink.

Senator Beck remarked: "Mighty good whiskey but it does have a strong taste of iron in it."

"You got to be wrong, Senator," his friend said. "This jugful was drawn from a barrel and there ain't no iron in the water of Peacock County. What do you think, Senator Blackburn?"

"I don't mind the iron taste in the whiskey," said Blackburn, "but I don't like the taste of leather in whiskey!"

"It's just not possible for this whiskey to have a leather taste," their friend exclaimed.

Together they went to the bar that had the barrel of whiskey from which the jug had been filled. They insisted that the whiskey be removed from the barrel and that a careful examination be made of its contents. To their amazement, they found one small piece of leather through which a carpet tack had been driven.

Always drink upstream from the herd!

(Cowboy advice)

They tell the story about the big celebration at which Al Smith, Jimmy Walker and several more of the old timers were at a convention and had decided to make a night of it at the conclusion of the first day's business. And they did make a night of it with several other important Democrats. The next day was a Catholic holy day, and Al Smith and Jimmy Walker knew they had to go to early Mass. All occupied the same suite of rooms so that when they tiptoed, both groggy and unsteady, through their shared suite — they passed Herbert Lehman and several others of the Jewish faith, all sleeping contentedly and peacefully.

Al Smith stopped and put his hand on Jimmy Walker's shoulder. "Jimmy," he whispered, "I sure hope we're right!"

Little girl: "Mother ... Daddy and I stopped at a place on the way home. I had a big glass of water and Daddy had only a small glass of water with an olive in it."

The sailor had been at sea for a long time. When he hit port, he headed straightaway for a tavern, entered and pointed at a gent laying prone on the floor, saying: "Give me a shot of that!"

It was time to close at Reilly's saloon and four old drunks, regular customers, were sprawled along the bar. Reilly gathered them up, took them outside to a cab and instructed the cab driver: "Drop the guy on the right off at 670 Park Avenue, the next one to him at 40 East 52nd Street, the third one at 811 Fifth Avenue and the fourth guy goes all the way up to Butler Hall at Columbia University." The taxi left but was back in a few minutes.

"Hey, Reilly!" the driver called. "Come on over and sort these guys out again ... I hit a bump on Madison Avenue."

Then there was the strange lush who wouldn't eat breakfast unless it had ice in it!

A famous actor was walking down the street one evening when a drunk halted him and asked, "C-can you tell me where'sh Alcoholics Anonymous, Mister?"

"You want to join?" asked the actor.

"H-Hell no ... I want to r-resign."

Jack says he's devoted to science as well as boozing. He says that he has willed his liver to science and claims that his drinking merely preserves it for that noble purpose!

Eddy Jenkins of Milwaukee, Wisconsin, was celebrating his sixtieth birthday with a huge party and ample booze. His wife, never a drinker, made a mistake and drank a glass of gasoline, thinking it was gin. When the party ended and all guests were about to leave and all were hiccuping, Mrs. Jenkins was ... honking!

Then there was the guy who was told by his doctor to eat more vegetables. And now he does just that ... he has three olives in every martini!

"You live here, alright, but you've come to the wrong place."

They'd only been married a few months and the bride complained bitterly to her husband about his drinking habits.

"What do you mean!" said the husband. "Sure I came in late last night but I didn't make any noise."

"No, you didn't, but the men who carried you in sure did."

Yes, death is at the bottom of the cup,
And everyone that lives must drink it up;
And yet between the sparkle at the top
And the blackness where lurks that bitter drop,
There swims enough good liquor,
Heaven knows,
To ease our hearts of all their other woes ...

William Dean Howells — 1837-1920

Whiskey: Trouble that's bottled. It is also the only enemy that man has managed to love.

The courthouse in Lincoln, Illinois has a large clock that is a historic masterpiece. They keep it lighted at night. One frowsy resident staggered up to a parking meter, dropped a dime in the slot, glanced up at the clock and yelled, "Holy shmokes, I'm ten pounds overweight!"

Prohibition: The period when Americans had been dried and found wanting!

"We'll take a parting drop together," the doomed man said to the executioner.

California Golden Era — 1860

They say that Toulouse-Lautrec, the famous French painter, drank too much. A friend castigated him for it: "How can you be such a fool as to drink so much!"

"I don't drink all that much," the artist responded, "I drink only very little ... but very often!"

Definition of a drunk: A guy who feels quite sophisticated ... but can't spell it.

There was a man in our town and he was wondrous
  wise.
He went into a barroom and drank a dozen ryes.
But when he saw what he had done, he cried with
  might and main.
And so he went across the street and started in again.

Prohibitionist: A spigot bigot. Also, a cellar-smeller.

AN ARGUMENT FOR PROHIBITION
The Antiseptic Pledge

"What? Leave a kiss within the cup,
  and I'll not ask for wine?"
"No, thank you, lady; I've read up
  about that kiss of thine."

I know it's full of leptothrix,
  Microbia and germs,
Who'll waft me toward the River Styx
  In scientific terms.

I know those micrococci wait
  For me to take some sips,
And if I thus should dare my fate,
  They'll camp out on my lips.

A myconostic cataclysm
  Will flood my tissues o'er,
A plymorphous-organism
  Will picnic in my gore.

The sphaero-bacteria
  Will win their one best bet,
And virulent diptheria
  Will be the least I'll get.

So, offer me a pledge to sup
  Of any vintage fine;
But leave no kiss within the cup,
  Or I'll not touch the wine.

"Simpkins, you should have fixed that leak hours ago."

"I always wake up at the crack of ice."

Joe E. Lewis

THE TEST

He is not drunk who, from the floor,
Can rise again and drink some more;
But he is drunk who prostrate lies,
And cannot drink, and cannot rise.

Eugene Field

"My dad was the town drunk. A lot of times that's not so bad — but New York City?"

Henny Youngman

─────────────

NAME YOUR POISON
by Ray Russell

Plain Talk does not a highball make, nor honest words a lush. Which, translated, means that we (yes, you and I) are probably inhibited about calling liquor and drinking and drunkenness by their real names.

You think not? Perhaps the point can be best illustrated by an imaginative, though not wholly imaginary, scene featuring — you guessed it: a certain girthful, sable-jawed author, now engaged in casting pearls before Hollywood swine, and sometimes vice versa.

We fade in as I enter my office in the writers' building of (Blank) Studios in my customary manner: palsied, yawning, skin chalky eyes bright as two raw oysters. Noting all this, my alert and pretty secretary asks, "Want some coffee?"

"Please."

"Large?"

"S'il vous plait."

"Black?"

"Por favor."

"And would you prefer Anacin, Bufferin or Excedrin?"

"One of each flavor, please."

"Chaser?"

"Alka-Seltzer on the rocks."

"Pretty rough night, eh?" she observes patronizingly.

"I really Tied One On," I admit.

"What? Aren't you the fellow who upbraided me the other day about the cowardly use of euphemism, circumlocution, synectoche, metonymy, and so on?"

"I'm the fellow. What about it?"

"Well, why do you say you Tied One On? Why don't

you simply admit you were drunk?"

"Because I *wasn't* drunk, smarty-pants, that's why. Not what *I'd* call drunk. I enjoyed a friendly Snort, yes, a Quick One just to Wet the Whistle; you know, One for the Road ..."

"You mean a glass of liquor?"

"I'll ignore that. There's nothing wrong with Bending the Elbow a bit with one's cronies to Repair the Tissues, getting together to Refresh the Inner Man by the time-honored custom of Hoisting a Few ..."

"Oh, now it's a few. A few what? A few Nips, Swigs, Shots, Slugs, Jolts?"

"If you will."

"Of Booze, Hooch, Sauce, Snake Oil, Redeye? Or maybe you only drank wine — oops, I mean the Grape."

"Are you *quite* finished?" I ask icily.

She isn't. "Was it an Eye Opener you had or a Pick-Me-Up? I suppose it was too early for a Nightcap or maybe you like to say the Cup That Cheers?"

"I wouldn't be caught dead saying the Cup That Cheers. And speaking of cups, Brighteyes, what about that coffee?"

"You wouldn't prefer the Hair of the Dog?"

"Woman! You try my patience! Begone!"

She vanishes, the fear of God plainly in her. I sink into my swivel chair, fall asleep and promptly dream an unusual dream. I dream a girl walks into my office carrying the complete works of Benjamin Franklin, in six volumes. Now, my secretary returns, and the sound of her voice awakens me abruptly:

"Here's your coffee. Also your pills. Also the complete works of Benjamin Franklin, in six volumes."

"I didn't ask for —"

"I suggest you read what he has to say in number twelve of the *Dogood Papers*."

"You. Are. Out. Of. Your. *Mind!* Benjamin Franklin on a Monday morning?"

"It's Tuesday afternoon."

She opens the *Dogood Papers,* and, with rapidly glazing eyes, I skim the words to which she points: "It argues some shame in the drunkards themselves, in that they have invented numberless words and phrases to cover their folly, whose proper significations are harmless, or have no signification at all. They are seldom known to be drunk, though they are very often Boozey, Cogey, Tipsey, Foxed, Merry, Mellow, Fuddled, Groatable, Confoundedly Cut, See Two Moons, or The Sun Has Shown Upon Them; they Clip The King's English, are Almost Froze, Feverish, In Their Altitudes, Pretty Well Entered —" At this point my eyeballs roll up into my skull of their own accord, and she says, alarmed:

"You worry me. I was going to lunch now, but I'm not sure I should leave you. Will you be all right?"

"Of course I'll be all right! Don't be so damned solicitous!"

"Well, you look sick."

"I am not sick. I have a Hangover, which is a very different thing. I'm a little Under the Weather, that's all."

"Just a touch of the Morning After?"

"That's the ticket. The usual Katzenjammers. The Horrors. A Big Head, nothing more. You go to lunch. Go right ahead and gorge yourself, that's quite all right; but in the spirit of reciprocal solicitude, I feel compelled to point out that you've been getting a trifle chunky around the middle; so it might be a good idea to go easy on the calories. Not that *I* mind, but sudden pudginess in girls is often misinterpreted, and people do talk. No, no, don't bother to thank me; it's part of my job to look after the welfare of my little charges. And, speaking of little charges, I assume your relief secretary — your petite, slender relief secretary — stands ready to defend the fort in your absence? Good, fine, excellent. Please inform her that I am not to be disturbed during the next hour for any reason. Got that straight? Swell. Ta-ta, sweetie, and as you walk into the commissary, avert your eyes from the sour-cream cheesecake with strawberry topping — it's murder on the shape."

Her exit is uncharacteristically silent. So is the hour that follows. No phone calls, no visitors, nothing to disturb my rest. I awake much refreshed and very hungry. I lift the phone to order a bit of lunch. It is dead. I jiggle the button. Nothing. Undaunted, I rise and walk to the door. It is locked. Giving vent to strong language, which I will not reproduce here, I fish my office key from my pocket and unlock the door. I am prepared to admonish the relief secretary, but she is not at her desk. In the carriage of the secretarial typewriter is a memo from secretary number one to secretary number two. I take the liberty of reading it:

"White Fang is in a filthy mood today," it reads, "and doesn't want to be disturbed 'for any reason.' I suggest you have the operator put a plug in the switchboard so he can't receive calls and so he won't be tempted to make any, either. We must save him from himself. By the same token, be so good as to lock his door so people won't be wandering in while he's snoring and drooling and making a spectacle of himself. And then, if I were you, I'd take the afternoon off, since there'll be nothing left to do. In the unlikely event that he outwits us and gets through to you, do not, under any circumstances, make reference to his delicate condition. If you find you absolutely must allude to it, for your own good, use only the following terms, which I have arranged in alphabetical order for your convenience: A Drop Too Much, Bagged, Barreled, Bit of a Glow On, Blasted, Blind, Blotto, Boiled, Buzzed, Cockeyed, Conked, Corked, Corned, Crocked, Feeling No Pain, Floating, Flying High, Fried, Gassed, Greased, Groggy, Half Shot, Has a Snootful, High, Inebriated, In His Cups, Intoxicated, Jagged, Juiced, Listing to the Leeward, Lit, Loaded, Looped, On a Bender, On a Spree, On a Tear,

On a Toot, Paralyzed, Petrified, Pickled, Pie-Eyed, Piffed, Pifflicated, Plastered, Plotched, Plotzed, Polluted, Puddled, Saturated, Seeing Double, Shellacked, Skunked, Smashed, Snoggered, Sozzled, Spiffed, Squiffed, Stewed, Stiff, Stinko, Stoned, Swacked, Tanked, Three Sheets to the Wind, Tiddly, Tight and Under the Influence. Those are off the top of my head, but if you need more, consult Ben Franklin's l2th *Dogood Paper* and *Roget's Thesaurus.* I don't want to give you the impression that our boy is a drunkard — he may be a Bibber, a Lush, a Rummy, a Toper, a Tippler, a Tosspot, a Souse, a Soak and a Sot; he may be Off the Wagon, but nothing worse than that. However ..."

My reading is interrupted by her return from lunch. Immediately I pantomime looking through her desk for rubber bands.

"They're in the top left drawer," she says flatly.

"Hm? Ah, there you are. Have you eaten your fill?"

"No," she pouts. "I decided you were serious about my getting chunky. I had a watercress salad."

"That's terrible! I apologize! You're not getting chunky at all!"

"You're just saying that."

"I'll prove it. Come out to dinner with me tonight."

"Why should I?"

"'Dost thou love life? Then do not squander time. Who pleasure gives shall joy receive'. That's why. You know who uttered that utterance?"

"Benjamin Franklin?"

"Absolutely correct. Pick you up about seven at your place. Better yet six-thirty. That'll give me time to sample your liquor before we —"

"Sample what?"

"What I mean is," I say loudly, to placate the gods of euphemism, "it's been a hell of a day, and I feel the need of a Wee Dram before dinner."

The Booze Book — Joy of Drink by Ray Russell
Playboy Press, 1974
Chicago, IL

"Jet set? No, I'm middle-class. I belong to the 'debt set.'"

"Excuse me, Mr. Bartender ... but do you serve women here?"

"Sorry but you'll have to bring your own."

———————

There was an old drunk called Hieronymus,
Who joined Alcohlics Anonymous;
But with liver disease,
The shakes and D.T.s,
The prognostication is ominous.

Ron Rubin

———————

"A drunken night makes a cloudy morning."

Cornwallis

A TALL COWBOY TALE

First cowboy: "I did own an ol' hoss one time that was about the dumbest critter I ever did see. I'll tell yuh what that fool horse did one night when I drunk too much likker and passed out in town. He picked me up and slung me on his back and carried me twenty miles to the ranch. When he got me there, he pulled off my boots with his teeth and nosed me into my bunk. Then he went to the kitchen, fixed up a pot of coffee and brung me a cup all fixed up with cream and sugar. Then the next day I had a hangover and he went by hisself and dug post holes all day so's the boss would let me sleep. When I woke up and found out what that fool horse had done, I cussed him for two days without stopping and wished him off on a greener*, which was passin' by. It was good riddance, too."

Second cowboy: "I'd say that wuz a pretty smart horse. What in the world did you get rid of him for?"

First cowboy: "Smart horse, you say? Who ever heard of a real cowboy usin' cream and sugar in coffee!"

*A sucker, patsy, green horn, dumbie, etc.

Arizona Nights
by Stewart Edward White, 1907

Did you know that the local bartenders have all threatened to strike? Yep! They want more overtime pay ... time and a fifth.

Two men, strangers, were sitting in the waiting room of the public library. One of the guys was pretty drunk and was having a hard time reading about birth and death statistics.

"Do you know," the drunk said, turning to the other man, "that every time I breathe a man dies?"

"A suggestion, Mister. Try chewing some gum!"

"Hey, Buddy, it's this way: down in Alabama we like our liquor hard and our women soft."

"Well, friend, up here in Illinois we like our liquor straight and our women curved!"

Two fellows, feeling their liquor, wandered into a public building. One asked the way to the cloak room and was told to take the first door on the left and go down three stairs. Due to his drunkenness, he opened the elevator door by mistake and fell three floors to the basement. His friend saw him leave, went to the door and called down, "What in hell are you doing down there?"

A voice floated up from the depths: "Hangin' by my coat. But be careful of that first step — it's a bastard!"

My husband is very good around the house ... there isn't a Martini or a Manhattan that he can't fix.

The policeman stopped to look down at a drunk on his hands and knees beneath a streetlight, peering around.

"Lose something?" the policeman asked.

"Yesh. Losht two bits!"

"Did you first miss it around here?"

"No, I losht it in lasht block."

"But why do you look for it here?"

"The light's mush better here."

"Did you hear about Peter? He was held up last night."

"I know. That's the only way he could get home."

"Of course your hotcakes tasted funny. You just ate the cork place mats."

It was the fourth time that Jerry Springer stood before the same judge on charges of intoxication.

"Your honor," said Jerry, "I promise you, give you my word that I ain't never gonna get drunk no more. No, Sir! I never said that before — that I'd take the pledge — but this time I say it and mean it!"

"May I ask when you made this decision to reform?"

"Two days ago. I spent two hours on my front lawn trying to kill the garden hose."

———

"The last time I swore off drinking," moaned Eddie Foy, "four bartenders sued me for non-support."

The defendant stood before the judge, weaving and grinning and hiccupping. The judge frowned down on him.

"Thomas," said the judge, "you've been brought before this court for excessive drinking."

"Thanks yer honor. Mighty nice. When do we start?"

"Now they tell us that whiskey and gasoline don't mix. What do you think?"

"They mix, all right, ... but it sure tastes lousy!"

Jack and Jill
Went in a still
To get some giggle-water.
Jack fell down and broke his crown
And Jill went home with another guy.

She drinks so much that her husband is afraid to let her light a match for a cigarette!

THE HELLBOUND TRAIN

Sung on a cow-camp near Pontoon Crossing, on the Pecos River, by a puncher named Jack Moore.

A Texas cowboy lay down on a barroom floor,
Having drunk so much he could drink no more;
So he fell asleep with a troubled brain
To dream that he rode on a hell-bound train.

The engine with murderous blood was damp,
And was brilliantly lit with a brimstone lamp;
An imp for fuel was shoveling bones,
While the furnace rang with a thousand groans.

The boiler was filled with lager beer,
And the Devil himself was the engineer;

The passengers were a most motley crew,—
Church member, atheist, Gentile, and Jew;

Rich men in broadcloth, beggars in rags;
Handsome young ladies, withered old hags;
Yellow and black men, red, brown, and white,
All chained together, — O God, what a sight!

While the train rushed on at an awful pace,
The sulphurous fumes scorched their hands and face;
Wider and wider the country grew,
As faster and faster the engine flew.

Louder and louder the thunder crashed,
And brighter and brighter the lightning flashed;
Hotter and hotter the air became,
Till the clothes were burnt from each quiverin' frame.

And out of the distance there arose a yell,
"Ha, ha," said the Devil, "we're nearing hell!"
Then, oh, how the passengers shrieked with pain,
And begged the Devil to stop the train.

But he capered about and danced with glee,
And laughed and joked at their misery.
"My faithful friends, you have done the work,
And the Devil never can a payday shirk."

"You've bullied the weak, you've robbed the poor;
The starving brother you've turned from the door;
You've laid up gold where the canker rust,
And have given free vent to your beastly lust."

"You've justice scorned and corruption sown,
And trampled the laws of nature down;
You have drunk, rioted, cheated, plundered, and lied,
And mocked at God in your hell-born pride."

"You have paid full fare, so I'll carry you through;
For it's only right you should have your due.
Why, the laborer always expects his hire,
So I'll land you safe in the lake of fire —"

"Where your flesh will waste in the flames that roar,
And my imps torment you forever more."
Then the cowboy awoke with an anguished cry,
His clothes wet with sweat and his hair standing high.

Then he prayed as he never had prayed till that hour
To be saved from his sin and the demon's power.
And his prayers and his vows were not in vain,
For he never rode the hell-bound train.

FIGHTIN' MAD

*Received from Miss Jean Beaumondy, Colorado
Springs Round-up, 1911. Jean was then the champion
girl trick roper of the world.*

I've swum the Colorado where she runs down close to
    hell;
I've braced the faro layouts at Cheyenne;
I've fought at muddy waters with a howling bunch of
    Sioux,
And I've eaten hot tamales in Cayenne.

I've rid a pitchin' bronco till the sky was underneath
I've tackled every desert in the land;
I've sampled four-X whiskey till I couldn't hardly see
And I've dallied with the quicksands of the Grand.

I've argued with the marshals of a half-dozen burgs;
I've been drug free and fancy by a cow;
I've had three years' campaignin' with the fightin', bitin'
    Ninth;
But I never lost my temper till right now.

I've had the yellow fever, I've been plugged full of
    holes,
I've grabbed an army mule plumb by its tail.
But I never was fightin', really downright fightin' mad,
Till you ups and hands me that damn ginger ale.

Reprinted from *Songs of the Cowboys*
By N. Howard Thorp.
University of Nebraska Press (Lincoln: 1984)

"I'm really thirsty! My tongue's hangin' out!"
"Oh golly ... I thought it was your tie!"

While riding the Amtrak passenger train to Chicago, an elderly lady noticed an obviously drunken passenger tearing paper into little pieces and throwing them out of the window.

"Pardon me, Sir," the lady asked, "would you mind explaining just what you're doing?"

"These shtrips sa-scares away all dem eleph-ph-phants."

"Elephants? Why I don't see any elephants," she said.

"Shee? It w-works, don't it!"

"A woman drove me to drink," W. C. Fields once said, "and I never even wrote to thank her for it."

W. C. Fields was told by his doctor that he wouldn't live six months more unless he quit drinking. Fields replied: "Y'know, Doc, that's exactly what a British doctor in Surrey told me twenty-five years ago. It's mighty good to discover that you doctors agree on something."

A friend said to W. C. Fields: "Mr. Fields, do you think your father would have approved of your drinking two quarts of whiskey a day?"

"I doubt it," said Fields. "He'd have called me a sissy!"

This fellow was really drunk and was driving down a one-way street the wrong way! An officer stopped him and asked him where he thought he was going!

"I ain't s-sure atall," the young guy replied. "But wherever it ish, I'm too late 'cause everybody ish already goin' h-home!"

I always know when my girlfriend drinks ... she starts to appear blurred.

A policeman was helping a drunk lying flat on the pavement, trying to get him on his feet. "Can you describe the man who hit you?" asked the cop.

"Sure," said the drunk. "I was doing just that when he hit me."

"I wonder if there's any lunch in the frig."
"Not a drop."

"Did I tell you about my huntin' trip in Alaska?" Sam asked George while both were seated at the bar.

"Nope. Ya didn't."

"Well, we were after grizzlies and, sure enough, early on, we spotted one and he came for me. He came lick-ety-split but I let him have it right between the yoors. Dropped him dead."

"Between the yoors? What's yoors?" George asked.

"Hey bartender," yelled Sam. "Thanks to my friend, I'll have a Scotch on the rocks."

Since I went to my doctor's office, I've been watching my drinking: I only drink in bars that have mirrors!

There was a young man of Porthcawl
Who thought he was Samson or Saul;
These thoughts so obscure
Were due to the brewer,
And not to his ego at all.

A. G. Prys-Jones

Then there was the fellow who drank eight cokes and burped 7-UP!

Old Mother Hubbard went to the cupboard
To get her poor self a shot
But when she got there, the cupboard was bare,
Cleaned out by her spouse, the sot.

It's a fact that many men who go into bars optimistically come out of them misty optically.

Dempster Mathews from Manhattan says he has the best cure for a hangover. Asked to tell us what it is, he replied, "You just squeeze the juice from a quart of bourbon and take it quick."

There was once a guy so dumb he took a ladder to the party because he heard the drinks were on the house.

Tom Henry was sitting at the bar when a fellow sat down beside him. "Say, you look familiar," the fellow said. "I know you. You're Charlie Gump."
"Nope. That's not my name, buddy."
"I'll be darned. Then you must have a double!"
"Thanks. Don't mind if I do. Bartender!"

"What'll ya have, Mister? Gin? Rum? Scotch? Brandy?"
"Yes."

The guy had fallen six stories and was just reviving on the ground with the help of a man who was holding a glass of water to his lips. "What's that you're giving me?" asked the fallen man.
"Water. You need it," said his rescuer.
"Water! How many stories would I have to fall to get a glass of whiskey?"

"Call things by their right names ... Glass of brandy and water! That is the current but not the appropriate name: ask for a glass of liquid fire and distilled damnation."

Gregory's *Life of Hall*

"The secret of a long life is to stay busy, get plenty of exercise and don't drink too much. Then again, don't drink too little."

Hermann Smith-Johannson

"If you are young and you drink a great deal, it will spoil your health, slow your mind, make you fat — in other words, turn you into an adult. Also, if you want to get one of those beefy, red and impressive-looking faces that politicians and corporation presidents have, you had better start drinking early and stay with it."

P. J. O'Rourke

Definition of a corkscrew: A mighty good key to unlock the store house of wit and the treasury of laughter, the door to fellowship, and a gate to pleasant foolishness.

On the chest of a barmaid in Sale
Were tattooed the prices of ale,
And on her behind
For the sake of the blind,
Was the same information in Braille.

Anonymous

"That is correct, sir. I did order a screwdriver. However,...!"

THE BATTLE OF THE KEYHOLES
by Don Marquis

The keyholes to the right of me
   Were dancing of a jig,
The keyholes to the left of me
   Were merry as a grig,
The keyholes right before my face
   Were drunk and winked at me,
And I stood there alone — alone.
   With one

           small
             key.

They frightened me, they daunted me;
   I turned back to the stair,
And faced nine keyholes pale and stern

That lay in ambush there.
Six keyholes on the ceiling sat,
　　Eight keyholes on the door,
And seven saddened keyholes lay
　　Hiccupping
　　　　　　on the
　　　　　　　　floor.

I crawled through one, I crawled through
　　two,
　　I crawled through keyholes three —
And then I saw a vistaed mile
　　Of keyholes waiting me!
"I will not crawl another yard
　　Through keyholes, though I die."
Oh, when my fighting blood is up
　　A Turk
　　　　　am
　　　　　　I.

They leapt at me, they flew at me,
　　They whistled as they came,
They gritted of their gleaming teeth,
　　They stung and spurted flame;
I put my back against the floor
　　And fought 'em gallantly —
But what could anybody do
　　With one
　　　　　small
　　　　　　　key?

Keyholes at the front of me,
　　And keyholes on the flank,
And as they rushed at me I smelled
　　The liquor that they drank;
Keyholes on my spinal cord,
　　And keyholes in my hair —
And with a "Heave together, boys!"

They rolled
    me down
        the stair.

It bumped me some, it bent me some,
  It broke a nose or two,
And when the milkman came, he said:
  "What Kaiser Belgiumed you?"
I says to him: 'It might have been
  The same with you as me
If you like me had had to fight
A gang of keyholes all last night
  With one
    small
      key.

Full and By, Being
A Collection of Verses in Praise of Drinking
edited by Cameron Rogers. New York:
Doubleday/Paget Co., 1925.

"I don't understand you Americans! First you say,
'Here's to you' ... and then you drink it yourself."

Defendant: "Judge, I believe in justice."
Judge: "Explain what you mean."
Defendant: "I believe in getting justice drunk as I can."

That guy drank so much beer at the party that when
he ate a pretzel, you could hear it splash.

"And so this jerk got careless and dropped a whole
bottle of whiskey on the floor."
  "Wow! I bet he feels awful about doing that."
  "Yep. But he'll be OK ... just as soon as they get all
the splinters out of his tongue."

Temperance official: "Sir. Why! Tell me why you drink whiskey!"

Drunk: "W-what elsh do y-you sug-g-gest I do with it?"

The guy was obviously hung-over as he staggered to the bar and groaned, "Gotta have something, anything to kill this hangover."

"Give me an idea what you need," the bartender said.

"Gimme ... gimme, somethin' tall ... colder'n hell ... and full of bourbon."

"Mister!" yelled the bartender, "you're talkin' about the woman I love!"

Alcohol — An excellent concoction to preserve almost anything you have ... except secrets!

Overheard at a drink-'em-dry session at the local bar:
"I sure do feel a heluva lot more like I do now than when I came in."

It has been said that it is possible for a fifth to go into three with none left over ... but ... maybe one to carry.

A terrorist banged into a bar shooting his pistol all the while and yelling, "All right now ... all you dirty bastards get outta here."

And did those customers fly! All were gone but one old geezer who sat calmly drinking at the bar. "What the hell are you doin' here?" yelled the terrorist.

"Just thinkin' that there sure were a lot of them, weren't there?"

"I've made it a rule never to drink by daylight and never to refuse a drink after dark."

H. L. Mencken — 1880-1956

Two guys were discussing their friend. "Have you noticed how he always fails to pay the check, lets somebody else do it?"

"Yeah, I've noticed that. I always said he had a reach impediment!"

A pink elephant is a beast of bourbon.

They tell the story about Robert Benchley, who was drinking martinis made with second-rate gin. A friend came by and said, "Bob, don't you know that drinking that rotten gin is slow death?"

"Yeah, I know it," said Benchley, "but I got plenty of time."

Why do they put Gideon Bibles in hotel bedrooms when where they need them is in the barrooms downstairs?

There were only a few days until Christmas, and Mrs. Brown was upset that her husband was taking so little interest in the cheery holiday. "I do wish you'd take more interest in making Christmas a glad occasion, Dear," she said to hubby. "Just look out the window and you can see the Petersons hauling into their home a lovely yule log."

"Yule log? That's no yule log, that's Peterson!"

I used to make good money but spent it on whiskey, all except what I wasted on groceries.

———————

Two men had grown up together and remained friends. One of them was a heavy drinker and the other admonished him on the evils of alcohol. "Lay off that stuff or it'll kill you, Pete," he said. "Why not water? Drink water when you're thirsty. It's the best of all drinks."

"What! Are you crazy!" his friend argued. "Water has killed lots more people than whiskey!"

"You're nuts!" his friend replied. "Give me an example."

"Well, to begin with, there was Noah and the flood."

———————

George is a very quiet guy unless he has too much to drink. Then he's as noisy as a jackass brayin' in a tin barn.

———————

The prisoner was very well-dressed and obviously a man of means. The judge looked him over and then asked the policeman, "Are you quite certain that this man was intoxicated when you arrested him?"

"Sure as shootin', Judge. He was really stewed."

"Tell me how you can be so positive."

"Well, Judge, he was dropping pennies in a mailbox on Second Street and then he looked up at the clock on the steeple of the public library and said: "Goodness gracious ... I've lost twenty pounds."

"If at first you don't succeed, try, try a gin!"

"One drop too much," murmured the repentant murderer as he dropped through the hangman's trap!

Reprinted from James Still. *The Wolfpen Notebooks*
Copyright © 1991, by The University Press of Ky,
by permission of the publishers.

The lecturer was a reformed alcoholic, and most of the town knew him. He was thundering away on the evils of alcohol and shouted, "There are eighty-six taverns, saloons and bars in this town. And I can tell you truthfully that I have never been in one of them!"

"Which one was that?" asked a voice from the audience.

Once I got sent up for making moonshine and that was mighty tough. But if they ever send me up again, it'll be for singin' too loud in church.

There was a new sign in the main room of the Lozenger Cocktail Lounge. It read, "You Are Requested Not To Rise And Stand While The Room Is In Motion!"

"My pleasures are buried deep," said the drunk as he saw his whiskey bottle tumble in to the lake.

Mister, when you buy a quart of liquor, you're buyin' a club to beat your brains out.

THE RIDDLE

Here's a riddle most abstruse:
Can you read the answer right?
Why is it that my tongue grows loose
Only when I grow tight?

UPPITY

An ex-coal miner from Kentucky went to Chicago to find work. He was a good-hearted fellow, but he wouldn't take anything off of anybody. He went into a bar that had a five-hundred-pound gorilla for a bouncer.

The Kentuckian drank a few and got to singing some of the old murder ballads. The owner of the bar got tired of his singing and unchained the gorilla, which went over and grabbed the miner and carried him outside.

There was a great commotion out there with a lot of banging and grunting, and finally the coal miner came back in and said, "Boy, give some people a fur coat, and they think they own the place!"

Hometown Humor U.S.A.
by Loyal Jones and Billy Edd Wheeler
August House, 1991: Little Rock, AR.

THE DRUNK BAR DARTER

This drunk happened to stagger into a restaurant where they were having a dart-throwing contest. The bartender said, "Mister, don't you want to try and win a prize here in this contest?"

He said, "Why, shore," and staggered over to throw a dart, and by some miracle hit the bull's eye. So they gave him the first prize, which was a turtle, and he staggered off with it.

Well, a few months later, he staggered into the same bar, and they were still having dart-throwing contests. Danged if he didn't hit the bull's eye again. The bartender said, "Hey, Mister, you look kinda familiar. Have you ever won a dart-throwing contest here before?"

He said, "Yes, Sir, I did."

The bartender went on, "Well, we don't want to give you the same prize you won before. What did you get?"

The drunk said, "The best I can remember, seems like was a roast beef sandwich on a real hard bun!"

Hometown Humor U.S.A.
by Loyal Jones and Billy Edd Wheeler
August House, 1991: Little Rock, AR.

IT'S A TOUGH JOB BUT ...

A man came home late rather intoxicated with a jar of moonshine in his hand. His wife was waiting at the door for him. She grabbed the jar and said, "I'm going to see what there is in this stuff that you like so much." She took two or three big swallows, lost her breath, coughed, turned red, and sputtered, "This stuff is terrible!" Her husband gazed her into focus and said, "And all this time, I'll bet you thought I was enjoying it."

Hometown Humor U.S.A.
by Loyal Jones and Billy Edd Wheeler
August House, 1991: Little Rock, AR.

Humpty Dumpty had a highball
Humpty Dumpty had a bad fall.
All the bromos and aspirins ten
Couldn't put Humpty Dumpty together again.

Toasts to Gladden a Drinker's Heart by an early American humorist, George Ade:

TOAST

Here's to the girls that call you honey
They drink your wine and spend your money
They put you to bed and hug you tight
And cross their legs and say good night.

Last night I hoisted twenty-three
Of these arrangements into me;
My wealth increased, I swelled with pride;
I was pickled, primed and ossified.
R-E-M-O-R-S-E!
Those dry martinis did the work for me.

Last night at twelve I felt immense;
Today I feel like thirty cents.

At four I sought my whirling bed,
At eight I woke with such a head!
It is no time for mirth or laughter —
The cold, grey dawn of the morning after.

If ever I want to sign the pledge,
It's the morning after I've had an edge;
When I've been full of the oil of joy
And fancied I was a sporty boy.
This world was one kaleidoscope
Of purple bliss, transcendent hope.
But now I'm feeling mighty blue —
Three cheers for the W.C.T.U.!
R-E-M-O-R-S-E!
The water wagon is the place for me.

I think that somewhere in the game,
I wept and told my maiden name.
My eyes are bleared, my copper's hot;
I try to eat, but I can not;
It is no time for mirth or laughter —
The cold, grey dawn of the morning after.

George Ade

He drinks so much whiskey that he didn't know the
water in his house had been cut off ... for two months!

H. L. Mencken (1880-1956) was an American journalist and essayist who was very critical of most aspects of American society. His essays scorned most institutions that Americans held dear and his prose was beautifully caustic about what most Americans take for granted ... religion, the American home, and the like. Here is an essay of his on drinking.

MEDITATIONS IN THE METHODIST DESERT
Portrait of an Ideal World

That alcohol in dilute aqueous solution, when taken into the human organism, acts as a depressant, not as a stimulant, is now so much a commonplace of knowledge that even the more advanced varieties of physiologists are beginning to be aware of it. The intelligent layman no longer resorts to the jug when he has important business before him, whether intellectual or manual; he resorts to it after his business is done, and he desires to release his taut nerves and reduce the steam-pressure in his spleen.

Alcohol, so to speak, unwinds us. It raises the threshold of sensation and makes us less sensitive to external stimuli, and particularly to those that are unpleasant. It reduces and simplifies the emotions. Putting a brake upon all the qualities which enable us to get on in the world and shine before our fellows — for example, combativeness, shrewdness, diligence, ambition — it releases the qualities which mellow us and make our fellows love us — for example, amiability, generosity, toleration, humor, sympathy.

A man who has taken aboard two or three cocktails is less competent than he was before to steer a battleship down the Ambrose Channel, or to cut off a leg, or to draw up a deed of trust, or to conduct Bach's B minor mass, but he is immensely more competent to entertain a dinner party, or to admire a pretty girl, or to *hear*

Bach's B minor mass. The harsh, useful things of the world, from pulling teeth to digging potatoes, are best done by men who are as starkly sober as so many convicts in the death-house, but the lovely and useless things, the charming and exhilarating things, are best done by men with, as the phrase is, a few sheets in the wind. *Pithecanthropus erectus* was a teetotaller, but the angels, you may be sure, know what is proper at 5 P.M. All this is so obvious that I marvel that no utopian has ever proposed to abolish all the sorrows of the world by the simple device of getting and keeping the whole human race gently stewed. I do not say drunk, remember; I say simply gently stewed — and apologize, as in duty bound, for not knowing how to describe the state in a more seemly phrase. The man who is in it is a man who has put all of his best qualities into his showcase. He is not only immensely more amiable than the cold sober man; he is immeasurably more decent. He reacts to all situations in an expansive, generous and humane manner. He has become more liberal, more tolerant, more kind. He is a better citizen, husband, father, friend. The enterprises that make human life on this earth uncomfortable and unsafe are never launched by such men.

They are not makers of wars; they do not rob and oppress anyone; they invent no such plagues as high tariffs, 100 per cent Americanism and Prohibition.

All the great villainies of history, from the murder of Abel to the Treaty of Versailles, have been perpetuated by sober men, and chiefly by teetotallers. But all the charming and beautiful things, from the Song of Songs to terrapin *á la Maryland,* and from the nine Beethoven symphonies to the Martini cocktail, have been given to humanity by men who, when the hour came, turned from well water to something with color in it, and more in it than mere oxygen and hydrogen.

H.L. Mencken
Prejudices: Fourth Series (1924)

"A jug and a book and a dame
and a nice shady nook for the same:
Said Omar Khayyam,
And I don't give a damn
What you say, it's a great little game!"

Edwin Meade Robinson

A fellow named Teddy Magee,
Rolling homeward one night from a spree,
Met a parson, who said,
"Ah, drunk again, Ted!"
"Sho'm I, Parson," gurgled Magee.

Anonymous

A censor, whose name was Magee
Suppressed the whole dictionaree;
When the public said, "No!"
He replied, "It must go!
It has alcohol in it, you see!"

Anonymous

There was a young druggist named Abel,
Who forgot to stick on the label;
It was poison within,
But was taken for gin:
He died at the end of a cable.

Anonymous

When that Seint George hadde sleyen ye draggon,
He sate him down furninst a flaggon;
And, wit ye well,
Within a spell
He had a bien plaisaunt jag on.

Anonymous

A man to whom illness was chronic
When told that he needed a tonic,
Said, "O Doctor dear,
Won't you please make it beer?"
"No, no," said the Doc, "That's teutonic."

Anonymous

At the bar in the old Inn at Leicester,
There's a beautiful barmaid named Heicester.
She gave to each guest
Only what was the buest,
And they all, with one accord did bleicester.

Anonymous

There was a young fellow named Paul,
Whose life was a sizzy high-ball;
But he drank them so fast
That they floored him at last,
And now his name's nothing at all.

Anonymous

All of the above limericks are from *Book of American Limericks*,
by Carolyn Wells.
New York & London: G.P. Putnam's Sons,1925.

"Early to bed and early to rise" ... Well, if you must, but you won't have any fun.

Charlie Brown had a treasured old-fashioned grandfather clock that had suddenly quit running. He picked it up and started down the street toward the watch repair shop. The clock was huge and heavy and Charlie was having a hard time carrying it when he approached a friend, who was obviously drunk. "Hey, Sh-sharlie," the drunk yelled. "Wouldn't it be eashier for you to own a wrisht watch?"

The guy was going hunting and made the mistake of finishing off a bottle of bourbon before his friends came for him. He staggered out to the car and the bunch took off for the lake and their duck blind. Now at the lake and in the duck blind, they eagerly awaited the ducks. Suddenly a single duck flies over and the drunk pulls up his gun, fires and down comes the duck.

"Wonderful," shouted a friend, "drunk as you are, you hit him kerblam! Great shot, Buddy!"

"Not sho dern great," the drunken guy replied. "With all those d-ducks up there, h-how could I miss!"

Can he make a dry martini? Well, I guess! When he makes one for you, you gotta eat it with a spoon!

The drunken guy was seated at the bar with his hands clasped. Every minute or so, he'd spread his thumbs and peer down into his cupped hands.

Curious, the bartender asked, "What ya holdin' in there, Buddy?"

"Take a guessh," said the lush.

"Bumblebee?"

"Nope," said the lush after taking a careful peek into his hands.

"Mouse?"

"Wrong again!"

"Then it's gotta be an elephant!"

The lush took another prolonged look and then asked, "What color?"

"Give an Irishman lager for a month, and he's a dead man. An Irishman is lined with copper, and the beer corrodes it. But whiskey polishes the copper and is the saving of him."

Mark Twain

Asked how he had fared during the four-week cure for alcoholism, the drunk replied, "It was gosh awful. I had to live on nothing but food and water!"

There was a young man so benighted
He didn't know when he was slighted;
He went to a party,
And ate just as hearty
As if he'd been really invited.

Frances Parkinson Keyes

"Claret is the liquor for boys, port for men; but he who aspires to be a hero must drink brandy."

Boswell's Life of Johnson

A famous comedian, Myron Cohen, told this story: "While traveling through the country, I've met a number of unusual drunks. One told me that he drank continually because he wanted to avoid hangovers. Another told me that he drank to forget. But the only thing he ever forgot was when to quit drinking. The third lush told me he came from an alcoholic family and that he was fourteen before he learned that toast was a piece of bread."

They say that a lot of men would live on booze alone if it weren't for pretzels!

"I DISAGREE WITH EVERYTHING YOU SAID EXCEPT FOR THE PART ABOUT BUYING ANOTHER ROUND."

The regular at the tavern was asked why he always closed his eyes when he drank his drink. He replied, "When I see good liquor like this it makes my mouth water. And I sure don't aim to have my drinks diluted."

"I am certain that the good Lord never intended grapes to be made into jelly."

Fiorello La Guardia

A couple of soused guys were weaving their way home one night and one of them said, "Shay, Buddy, won't your w-wife hit the ceiling when you get home tonight?"

"S-she p-probably will," he replied. "She's a lousy shot."

Did you hear about the college student, a young fellow who'd been drunk since his sophomore days in high school? Well, the guy was voted by his fellow classmates, the student most likely to dissolve.

A fellow came into the bar, sat down and ordered a martini. Before he drank it, he removed the olive and put it in a small glass jar. He ordered several more martinis, always removed the olives and put them in the jar. Observing this odd behavior, one man remarked to another, "Did you ever see anything so curious? I wonder why he does that!"

"Because his wife sent him out for a jar of olives!"

"I never let anybody beat me to the punch," said the old comedian, Ed Wynn, "especially if it's been spiked!"

It's been said that a lot of wives whose husbands come home half shot, feel like finishing the job.

There was a habitual drunk who staggered home one night, groped about and finally ended up in the shower with the water turned on full force. The sound of running water awakened his wife and she came to the door and was furious at the mess he was making.

"You jerk! Coming home drunk and flooding the bathroom ..."

"You're a hun-n-ndred pershent right, Honey," he said, "but please let me in 'cause itsh raining like hell out here."

The horse and mule live 30 years
And nothing know of wines and beers.
The goat and sheep at 20 die
And never taste of Scotch or Rye.
The cow drinks water by the ton
And at 18 is mostly done.
The dog at 15 cashes in
Without the aid of rum and gin.
The cat in milk and water soaks
And then in 12 short years it croaks.
The modest, sober, bone-dry hen
Lay eggs for nogs, then dies at 10.
11 animals are strictly dry;
They sinless live and swiftly die;
But sinful, ginful, rum-soaked men
Survive for three score years and ten.
And some of them, a very few,
Stay pickled till they're 92.

Anonymous

He's drunk constantly. Why, they had to burn down
the tavern to get him home.

A DRUNKARD'S ODE

How well do I remember, t'was in the late November,
I was walking down the street quite full of pride,
My heart was all a-flutter as I slipped down in the
    gutter,
And a pig came there and laid down by my side;
And as I lay there in the gutter, all too soused to even
    mutter
A lady passing by was heard to say:
"One may tell a brute that boozes by the company he
    chooses,"
Hearing this the pig got up and walked away.

"I feel as though someone stepped on my tongue with muddy feet."

W. C. Fields

It's an interesting literary journey to travel back to turn-of-the-century America and see the saloon and its appendages (gambling joints, houses of prostitution, etc.). Perhaps one of the most remarkable and interesting customs of that time was the free food that the saloons offered with your drink. George Ade (1866-1944), a distinguished newspaper reporter and author of many books concerning his times, wrote one revealing, humorous book called *The Old Time Saloon.* The following description of the famous "free lunch," served at most big town saloons in the 1890s and early 1900s, is described in his book. Here it is — a phenomenon of the American past — the free lunch (today you might get peanuts!)

THE FREE LUNCH

NOW we come to a subject regarding which many illusions need to be dispelled. Meaning, of course, the free lunch. No doubt you have come across the legend that during the Golden Age of King Alcohol any willing buyer in any saloon could get for absolutely nothing all of the important food items for which Delmonico and Sherry charged large prices.

It is true that in any of the larger and more popular and prosperous drinking resorts with cathedral architecture and all the mixers wearing lodge emblems, the long table across from the bar showed a tempting variety of good things to eat. There might be salted nuts, roast turkey, a spiced ham, a few ribs of beef, potato salad, potato chips, ripe olives, sandwiches, Herkhimer County cheese, summer sausage and napkins. The waiter in the white apron would slice off anything the customer seemed to crave and pile up a grand variety on a plate, especially if his palm had been crossed with silver. The seemingly boundless generosity of a few of the money-making emporiums is still talked about and happy memories of a sentimental character linger with the more elderly soaks who now submit to the extortions of the speak-easy.

Other bars not so generous would offer free bowls of soup every noon. Many would have free-lunch specialties for every day in the week, as, for instance: Monday, hot frankfurters; Tuesday, roast pork; Wednesday, roast mutton; Thursday, Irish stew; Friday, baked fish and dressing; Saturday, roast beef and mashed potatoes; Sunday, dry crackers. Many were wide open on the Sabbath day and others merely had the curtains down and the side entrance unlocked, but there seemed to be a general understanding that patrons would eat at home on the day of rest, which wasn't always so restful if enough of the gang got together.

Any open-hearted benefactor who began the practice of giving away liberal portions of food to his friends and customers was invariably annoyed by visits from undesirables pretending to be friends and also by ravages on the free-lunch counter by low-down deceivers who had not passed any money over the bar. The code governing the privileges of the free-lunch department was exacting and was observed by the genteel trade even if ignored by tourists, who happened to be passing through the city on foot, and other unfortunates who had hit the grit. Hunger will overcome modesty and weaken self-respect. The stony-broke who had seen better days would have died rather than go to a back door and beg for a hand-out but he had no scruples against cleaning the lunch counter, trying to watch the ryebread, the Limburger cheese, the bar-keep and the door leading to the street, all at the same time.

Gentle methods were not employed in dealing with the drop-ins who moved direct to the food-trough instead of proceeding to the bar and giving the house some trade. Many of the larger places employed special "bouncers" who watched all who came in and made sure that only the buyers were having their plates filled with a menu which would now cost one dollar at any hotel of the first magnitude.

Both the bouncer and the barkeep had to exercise a nice sense of discrimination in sorting out the willing spenders from the dead beats. They had to be careful and they were. The shabby person who sidled up to the array of eatables and was pronging in all directions and trying to get a couple of square meals for an investment of nothing whatsoever, was out of luck when apprehended.

The Argus-eyed server of drinks could splash out orders to eight customers simultaneously and, at the same time, check up on six free-lunchers and spot a "ringer" with the sureness of a bird-dog flushing a quail. The reason why vagrants so seldom put over their cadging operations was that they looked guilty.

The bartender always acted promptly but he was at a great disadvantage. By the time he had secured the bung starter and run all the way to the end of the bar and turned the corner, the hobo had made a flying get-away through the swinging doors and was headed toward the setting sun.

It was the floor-walking bouncer who made life a hell for the boys who were hungry but broke. He had a way of sneaking up from behind. His favorite hold was one hand on the collar and the other taking up the slack in the trousers and when he threw a non-producer for a loss of twenty yards, the victim was out of play. He never came back for more.

Believe it or not, bouncing became a fine art and out of the thousands and thousands of American citizens who were heaved into the street from saloons, dance halls, hotel lobbies and all-night restaurants, it is not on record that the bouncers made one single mistake. In the large and busy eating places which catered to night-hawks of every description the waiters were carefully recruited from the prize-ring stables. Any one of them had tattoo marks on him and could bend a horseshoe. The staff in the famous nocturnal resort known as "Jack's," just across from the New York Hippodrome, was drilled as carefully as West Point cadets. Those waiters were the friendliest eggs in the world until someone started to rough it up.

Let us pause for a minute to inquire why it is that the sons of the rich, who received early training from tutors and governesses, and then attended the best prep schools and, later, received degrees from the more important universities, are usually the ones who wait to lick policemen and cabmen, break glassware and forcibly drag chorus girls away from some other table. It is so today and it was just as much so in the halcyon days and nights when "Jack's" was always jammed until broad daylight. The collegians, and others who could not breathe the night air without becoming belligerent, seemed to think that "Jack's" was just the place in which to stage a battle. When fists began to fly and furniture was crashing, the waiters closed in swiftly from all direc-tions. The teamwork was wonderful. They gave every disturber of the peace what was known as the "bum's rush." All of the gallant youths who had been fighting to win the approval of blondes or brunettes, or both, found themselves in the middle of Sixth Avenue, looking up at the stars.

Unfortunately for the retail trade, not every saloon could hire a trained bouncer, and the busy barkeep was handicapped by being compelled to cover a lot of dis-tance, after securing the bung-starter and declaring war. The trade boasted very few Malachy Hogans. Malachy kept a place on Clark Street, Chicago, half way between the Grand Opera House and the Sherman Hotel. He could vault over the bar and light on an unwelcome caller with the destructive effect of a horse lying down on a butterfly. He had to inspect the line coming in at the door because his free lunch serving-table was famous for variety and quality. A high-brow editorial writer one day complimented him on his food service.

"That's funny," said Malachy. "Yesterday I was playing pinochle in the back room with Collector of Port Russell, Archbishop Feehan and Maggie Cline an' they all raved about the lunch, same as you."

Malachy said this to a relative of Martin Russell — one of the most dignified, scholarly and well-behaved gentlemen in the city — and the relative walked out, horrified and puzzled.

The raiding of free lunches became almost a steady job and a regular trade for flophouse derelicts and nogoods who were on their uppers, so a great many saloons adopted the rule of giving out food from the bar or handing the customer a ticket which he could take across to the food department and exchange for a bowl of soup.

Here was a sign that you saw behind many a bar:
A fried oyster, a clam
or a hard-boiled egg with
every drink.

This sounds incredible, but there was a basement place under one corner of the McVicker Theatre Building, Chicago, which specialized on selling beer customers huge wedges of pie at five cents the wedge. You would naturally believe that about a gallon of beer in combination with apple, huckleberry or cocoanut pie might form a dangerous explosive. Nevertheless, many of the boys liked pastry with their suds. The show window of that highly-perfumed cellar resort under good old McVicker's always had a vast array of pies arranged in stacks so high that a greyhound couldn't have jumped over them.

Free lunch became an institution because of the well-known zoölogical fact that certain kinds of food promote thirst and any malt fluid with a sharp tang to it encourages hunger. The more lunch the beer hounds consumed the greater was their enthusiasm for salty food, and the more pretzels and sardellen they gobbled up, the more enduring became the thirst. The net result was a positive demonstration of the fact that the textbook on physiology, which said that the total capacity of the human stomach was three pints, was simply groping in the dark. It was offering an obsolete theory instead of recognizing plain facts.

One whole chapter might be devoted to that vitrified and 8-shaped article of food known as the pretzel. Because it was so glossy and offered so much resistance to bad teeth, many supposed that it belonged to the mineral kingdom. "Biff" Hall, President of the famous Turn-Over Club, discovered that nearly all of the pretzels consumed in the middle west were made at a foundry on the North Side, in Chicago. He visited the pretzel mill and saw the whole works in operation. The handcarved wooden patterns were imbedded in the moist sand of the molding boxes and then lifted out, leaving hollow spaces into which a molten fluid could be poured as it came whitehot from the crucibles. When the pretzels had hardened so that they could be lifted from the sandboxes they went from the main foundry to another department in which salt was sprinkled on them. Then they went to the cooling room and remained there until they were ready to be carried by overhead cranes to the varnishing shop. After they had acquired the proper

lustre they were ready to be crated and sent to the
saloons. Those who clamor for the return of beer say
that pretzel foundries cannot be re-opened and run at a
profit unless the Volstead Act is modified. The attempt to
keep pretzel mills going as noodle factories has not been
successful, because the old equipment cannot be uti-
lized. Noodles must be snipped off by hand, after the
dough has been worked into an elastic condition, where-
as the pretzel has to be cast in hollow molds, the same
as automobile parts.

Probably the most valuable of all the thirst-provoking
items included in the average free lunch was the limp,
silver-coated minnow called the "sardel," a relative of the
sardine. Always it was known by the German plural for
the name, which was "sardellen." The aristocratic sardine, immersed in olive oil and coming in small cans,
was too expensive to be set out in large platters.
Furthermore, olive oil counteracts the influence of alcohol. This important discovery was made by the U. S.
Navy. But the sardellen, saturated with brine and probably sold by the hogshead, became one of the staple
stand-bys of every saloon catering to a reliable beer
trade. They were saltier than the Seven Seas and were
served whole. No one had tampered with the heads,
tails or interior arrangements. They were in great favor
because a patron after he had taken a couple of them,
draped across a slab of rye bread, had to rush to the bar
and drink a lot of beer to get the taste out of his mouth.
The sardellen were more than fish. They were silent
partners.

As a matter of cold truth, the average free lunch was
no feast for Lucullus or "Diamond Jim" Brady, but a
stingy set-out of a few edibles which were known to give
customers an immediate desire for something to drink.
The idea was to set out as much as possible at small
expense. Rye bread was always present. Right in the
center of the soiled tablecover you might have found a

bowl of baked beans and alongside of it a glass of troubled water and in the glass were immersed several forks which, the evidence indicated, had been used in hoisting beans. The thin slices of limber yellow cheese were flanked by a smeary pot of brown mustard with a paddle in it. The common "boloney," which used to sell by the yard instead of the pound, was over-seasoned with pepper, for a definite reason. There might be spring onions and radishes but only when they were plentiful and cheap. Fortunately there was no closed season for dill pickles. In a German place you might find blut-wurst or blood sausage, a dainty made up of coagulated blood which had not been cooked but which had been shot full of salt and black pepper. Or the hard and leathery cervelat or summer sausage. The longer it was kept, the more petrified and tasty it became.

The regulars who went around shopping sometimes discovered pickled pig's feet, but they were more apt to find sauerkraut. If you do not find ripe olives and veal cutlets and imported Gruyere on this list, remember we are describing a saloon and not a "buffet."

Mention must be made of one of the stars of the group, ranking well up with the pretzel and the sardel. Referring, of course, to your old playmate known as the Dried Herring, alias the Black-Eyed Susan, alias the Blind Robin. He was withered, and shriveled and warped, with dead eyes and tail awry, but the devotees who were fond of former fish that had been imperfectly preserved in salt, preferred him to terrapin. He can still be found at a delicatessen store but his social eminence has departed in spite of the fact that he is first cousin to the patrician kippered herring, known throughout Great Britain as "the drunkard's breakfast."

That's all there is to tell about the typical free lunch. It was just a collection of culls and the main idea was not to provide nourishment but merely excite an undying thirst. The usual free lunch was not calculated to arouse the enthusiasm of an epicure. The spread represented a small investment and would not have been alluring to a teetotaler but the boys nibbled at it between schooners. When a beer fiend was gulping them down, one after another, he would eat anything except hay.

Reprinted from *Old Time Saloon*
by George Ade.
New York: Richard R. Smith, Inc., 1931

"Now that's what I call a hunting jacket!"

I drink only when I'm alone ... or with somebody.

THE WEEKLY NEWSPAPER — PIONEER POETS

I said to my nose, Oh Nose, Red Nose;
Will you say to me, honor bright,
What the hidden cause in the matter was
That you came to such a sight?

I said to my nose, Oh Nose, Red Nose;
You shame me at every turn,
And whene'er I am in the hot old sun,
You blister and blaze and burn.

I said to my nose, Oh Nose, Red Nose;
Is there any relief in reach?
Is there any old dye that I can buy
That will work as a nasal bleach?

The red nose lifted itself a notch,
And answered me, "Aber nit:
If you drink less grog and more water, hog,
It would whiten me up a bit."

"Liquor talks mighty loud w'en it git loose from de jug."

Joel Chandler Harris

"Howdy, Paul ... how'd you spend the weekend?"
"I went fishing. Fished through the ice."
"Yeah? What were you fishin' for?"
"Olives."

There's a joint in Peoria, Illinois that has this sign over the bar: "OUR MARTINIS ARE SO DRY THEY'RE DUSTY!"

Two twins, quite identical, sat at the bar. They were dressed exactly alike and appeared duplicates in every way. A drunk came unsteadily into the bar and stared at them. He kept staring at them, then rubbing his eyes, then again stared at them.

"It's all right, Mister. You aren't seeing things, we really are twins."

The drunk blinked a couple of times, then said, "All four of you?"

"The body was rich in lead but too badly punctured to hold whiskey." Cowboy's condition, stated by a friend.

A gentleman had been coming to the bar for weeks. He always ordered two bourbons on the rocks. This had gone on for some weeks when the bartender suggested to him: "Sir, why don't you order only one drink at a time? When you order two, the ice melts in one of them and dilutes it."

"Thanks for the suggestion," the man said, "but I do this for my business partner. We were together for years and afterward always had a drink together. We made a pact that if one of us died, the other would continue our arrangement and order a second drink in the other's memory."

"That's a might touching story, Sir. I understand now."

Some weeks later, the gentleman ordered only one drink at a time and the bartender was curious. "Sir?" he asked, "Now you order only one drink at a time. Did your partner return to earth from the hereafter?"

"Oh, no," the man replied. "It's just that now I'm on the wagon."

A little girl came home from school, and when she kissed her mother she smelled liquor. "Hey, Mom," she shouted. "You're wearing Daddy's perfume!"

"May I say, Susan, that your husband is really tremendously overweight. Why don't you put him on a serious diet?"

"We've tried everything," she replied. "The problem is that Harry thinks a balanced diet is holding a martini in each hand!"

"Did you hear about Pete? He lost his glasses."
"Golly gee! Now he'll have to drink out of the bottle."

The limerick is one of the oldest forms of poetry genius: tomfoolery. And they are fun!

A happy young lass from Terry,
On beer was loving and merry,
She played with sin,
On whiskey and gin,
But was rigid and frigid on sherry.

BEST OLD FELLER YOU EVER SAW
by Paul Patterson

Born On A West Texas Ranch, Paul Patterson spent most of his youth working as a cowboy in the country just east of the Pecos River. After service in World War II and a brief interlude as a disc jockey in Fort Worth, he became a high school history teacher, settling finally at Crane, where he taught school for a living and wrote humorous tales about the cow country for fun. He is a legitimate humorist with a sharp eye for character and a keen ear for cowboy talk. His characters are authentic and are sometimes given their right names — a fact which makes him a historian as well as a humorist.

Joe Thorp's Daddy owned a little spread and a big family of little kids, all of which he ran out of Mertzon a ways. Even in those days of plenty of cowboys it was hard to get a good man, especially on a little spread. It seems that the good hands all gravitated to the OH Triangle, the Bar S or to where the big happenings were.

The help he managed to pick up were generally no count. Always their hands seemed too soft for a crowbar and too stiff for a cow's teat. And these cowboys were generally too hard on horses and too easy on post hole diggers.

Finally, in town old man Thorp picked up a hand, not young. He didn't look like much — shabby, scrawny, and run down at the heel. Old man Thorp worried at first, but as it turned out he had landed him a crackerjack good hand. There wasn't a lazy bone in his body, and, what's more, best old feller you ever saw. Easy on horses and kind to the milk cows, he knew how to take care of a team and could do anything there was to do around a ranch. He could even farm if it came to that. He was as handy inside the house as on the outside — he could cook, wash dishes, and scrub. And it wouldn't have surprised old man Thorp if this good old man had been able to knit.

On top of that, the old man didn't use tobacco to excess, didn't cuss, was neat in all his habits, and patient with all the kids, which latter, to old man Thorp, was a miracle in itself. His wants were simple and his needs were few.

"Anything atall you might want from town?" was always Mr. Thorp's question when he went in.

"Nope, not a thang," was always the old man's reply.

"They's bound to be somethin' I can get for that good old man," Mr. Thorp repeated to himself one day on the way to town.

Eureka! He believed he had found it. Maybe that good old man might like a little toddy of a morning.

"That's it! Never seen a feller yet — even some preach-ers — as wouldn't take a little nip of toddy of a mornin'. But I'm purt' near afraid to ask that good old man."

But by the time Mr. Thorp had gotten back to the ranch he was positive in his own mind that that good old man wouldn't be offended by his offering.

"Since you never want anythin atall for yoreself, I took it upon myself to bring you somethin' as might be good for you. I hope I ain't mistaken," he said, delivering a quart to that good old man.

It wasn't until that good old man had scared the chick-ens out of thirty days of laying, crippled a milk cow or two and chopped down the gallery posts, that old man Thorp realized he was mistaken.

Shortly thereafter Mr. Thorp was flogging it back to town with that quart of whiskey, most of which was sur-rounded by that good old man — the best old feller you ever saw — nearly.

From Pecos Tales. Austin: Encino Press, 1967. Publications of the Texas Folklore Society, no. 31, pp. 17-18.

I'm for temperance: Drunk or sober.

Northern Pennsylvania saying

Oh many a peer of England brews
Livelier liquor than the muse,

And malt does more than Milton can
to justify God's ways to man

Ale, man, ale's the stuff to drink
For fellows whom it hurts to think.

A. E. Housman — 1859-1936

GASPIRTZ

"SAM DOESN'T GIVE A DAMN."

The fellow from Chicago was on his first trip to New Orleans, visiting a friend. He was shown the guest room and was preparing for bed when the maid came in. "My, you have lots of mosquitoes down here," he said to her.

"We sure does," she replied.

"Well, don't they bother my friend Elmer? In this house all the time?"

"You'd think so," she replied, "but the first part of the night, the boss is too full to pay attention to the skeeters and the last half of the night, them skeeters is too full of the boss to pay 'tention to ... him!"

There is absolutely no sense in trying to drown your sorrows because they are the world's champion swimmers!

The guy had been drinking at the bar for over an hour. Finished with four beers, he walked up to the bartender and asked, "I been wondering, just how many kegs of beer do you sell each week?"

"Well, it's something around eighty kegs, Mister."

"Let me tell you how you can double that figure," said the customer.

"Please do," replied the bartender.

"Just fill the glasses," replied the customer.

One of the best ways for a woman to look her best is to give her man three cocktails.

The entire barroom was astounded when this chimpanzee walked into the tavern, up to the bar, sat down and ordered a cocktail.

Finished with his drink, the chimp stood, laid down a twenty dollar bill and waited. The bartender took the money and returned a ten dollar bill. The chimp took the money and turned to leave. "Hey!" the bartender called, I'm sorry I seemed so shocked when you came in but you're the first chimpanzee we ever had in here."

"I shouldn't wonder," replied the chimp "especially when you charge ten dollars for a drink!"

If all the college students in the United States were laid end-to-end, it'd take a lot of liquor!

"Hey Bartender ... was I in this joint last night and did I spend thirty bucks on drinks?"

"You sure were and did, Sir."

"What a relief. I thought I'd lost it."

W. C. Fields

"Hey, Buddy?" the drunk asked of the other drunk sitting next to him at the bar. "Is the sun setting or rising?"

"I really c-can't say. I d-don't live around here."

Whatever is in the heart and mind of a sober man is in the mouth of a drunkard.

"I had a bad cold and a fellow told me the best thing for it was to drink a quart of whiskey and go to bed. On the way home, another fellow told me the same thing. That made half a gallon."

Mark Twain

"I heard you got fired for attending your uncle's funeral, George."

"Yeah, my boss got mad 'cause I took three days off for the funeral."

"Yeah? Well, tell me ... why did you need three days for the funeral?"

"My uncle was a heavy drinker. He was cremated and it took us three days to put out the fire."

Glasses sure are becoming to some folks 'til they start drinking from them.

LITTLE BROWN JUG

Me and my wife and a bob-tailed dog,
Crossed the river on a hickory log,
My wife fell in, the dog got wet,
But I hung on to my little brown jug, you bet!

Chorus

Ha, ha, ha, you and me!
Little brown jug, don't I love thee?

When I am working on my farm,
I take little brown jug under my arm,
Put him under a shady tree
Little brown jug, don't I love thee?

Chorus

If I had a cow that gave such milk,
I'd dress her in the finest silk,
I'd feed her on the choicest hay
And milk her sixty times a day.

Chorus

The rose is red, my nose is too,
The violets blue and so are you,
And yet I guess, before I stop,
I'd better take one last drop.

It's been said that alcohol is an excellent preservative for many things ... but not secrets!

The drunk who takes one more "for the road" will probably have a highway cop for a chaser.

The drunk got into the cab and said, "Driver, take me t-to the G-Girly Girl Club."

The driver turned and said, "Mister, you ARE at the Girly Girl Club!"

"Thanks," said the drunk, getting out. "Nexsht time d-don't drive sho fasht!"

"Alcohol is a very necessary article ... It enables Parliament to do things at eleven at night that no sane person would do at eleven in the morning."

Johnny Pearson staggered upstairs and crawled into bed, barely able to make it, he was so drunk. Then, of all nights for it to happen — the phone rang. He staggered out of bed, went to the phone, answered it, and heard this: "Mr. Pearson, I'm your neighbor and if your dog doesn't quit all that barking, I'll call the police."

The next night at the same time, at 2 A.M., Johnny called his neighbor. "Sir," he said when the neighbor answered, "I don't have a dog."

Two heads are better than one, unless they have hangovers.

Two guys were out deer hunting and hadn't had any luck all day. Finally, a deer appeared within easy range and one fellow took two quick shots. But before he could get the cork back in the bottle, that danged deer was gone!

Customer: "I'm sure sorry, bartender, but I've got only enough money to pay for my drinks. I've got none left for your tip."

Bartender: "Let me have a look at that bill, Sir. I'll add it up again."

"The only reason I drink is because when I am sober I think I am Eddie Fisher."

Eddie Fisher

A preacher was delivering his Sunday sermon when a drunk wandered into the church and sat down in a back row. He was holding a bottle of whiskey and swigging away on it. Suddenly, a young lady in the balcony stood to arrange her dress, stumbled and fell out of the balcony. Luckily, she grabbed a hanging chandelier and held on.

The preacher, seeing her predicament, said, "Anybody who looks up that young lady's dress will be stricken blind by the lightning of God."

"Well," said the drunk who was not at all religious, "I'll close jush one eye an ... an take a shance on the uh-uh-uhther."

Alcohol is an extremely stable chemical ... until you drink it.

"I IGNORE HIM! HE'S JUST TRYING TO BE THE CENTER OF ATTENTION."

A drunk collapsed on the street in Chicago. It was the hottest day of the year and an old lady joined the crowd gathered around the fallen drunk. She said, "Give him a drink of whiskey."

Another person said, "Give him a drink of water."

Still another person said, "Smelling salts would be best."

The old lady repeated, "Give him a drink of whiskey!"

"Wrap his head in a towel soaked in ice water," said another.

"Will you people s-shut up," the drunk moaned, "and just do what the old l-lady tells you!"

"They drink with impunity ... or anybody who invites them."

Artemus Ward — 1834-1867

"The trouble with the world is that everybody in it is three drinks behind."

Humphrey Bogart

John Petefish's most compelling wish was to live to be a hundred years old. He went to his physician to find out what he should do in order to reach that age. The doctor told him that he must quit drinking, must not have even a single drop of whiskey, gin or the like if he hoped to reach the age of one hundred.

"But Doctor," asked John, "Are you sure I'll make it if I cut out all drinking?"

"I can't promise," said the Doctor. "But I can promise it'll sure seem like it!"

It's easier to stand the smell of liquor than to listen to it.

"The only way to keep your health is to eat what you don't want, drink what you don't like, and do what you'd rather not."

Mark Twain — 1835-1910

When your companions get drunk and fight, take up your hat and wish them good night.

The Hanson Window Manufacturing Company in Iowa City, Iowa, was having trouble with pigeons. A hundred of them would perch above the front door, on the top ledge of the building and scatter droppings all over the sidewalk. An employee suggested a way to get rid of them. "Take a bushel of cracked corn, soak it in bourbon so the birds get drunk and they'll stay away from your building."

The company tried it. But the problem was that the day after they put out the mixture, four hundred pigeons showed up!

Knowledge and alcohol have at least one thing in common ... a little bit of it is sometimes as bad as too much.

Sometimes a silent defense is the best kind. Witness the yardman who was accused by his employer, a sharp-tongued lady, of being a drunkard because she had seen his wheelbarrow parked outside a tavern.

The worker said not a word but, the same night, he placed his wheelbarrow outside her door and left it there all night.

Scientific fact: Nothing is more soluble in alcohol than a man's conscience.

A friend asked David Letterman if he knew of any girls who didn't drink, smoke, swear or have any other bad habits.

"What for?" David replied.

There are many virtues that can be preserved in alcohol, but dignity is not one of them.

"Drinking is the curse of the country!" a minister thundered.

"Why so?" he was asked.

"Because it lets you foolishly argue with your neighbor and it wisely makes you shoot at the tax collector ... but <u>miss</u> him!"

A drunkard is like a whiskey-bottle, all neck and belly and no head.

CAUTION

Saint Patrick was a gentleman
Who through strategy and stealth
Drove all the snakes from Ireland —
Here's a bumper to his health.
But not too many bumpers,
Lest we lose ourselves, and then
Forget the good St Patrick
And see the snakes again.

Unknown

I WONDER HOW THAT BEER TASTED
by Chris Morley

Back in the days of the Depression, I went to work for the D&H Railroad as a messenger boy. I was about ten years old and used to run around delivering telegrams and messages to the mills in town.

I'd often sit in the corner of the station listening to the old timers, some of whom were Civil War veterans and they'd be telling war stories and jokes, lots of jokes. Some of those jokes might not have been funny at the time, but looking back on them, you couldn't help but laugh.

There were these two fellows who worked in the stable of the old Lincoln Hotel. They liked to drink and they didn't like to do much work. They'd wash down the horses and then take the money and buy beer.

On one slow day, with no money in hand, one of the men said to the other, "Go get that horse sponge and wring it out well." They pushed that sponge down into a crock and took it round to one of the taverns to have it filled. After it was full, they turned their pockets out but they couldn't produce a dime. No money, No Beer was the motto of the day and the barkeeper dumped the brew back into the barrel and handed them back their crock.

When they got back to the stable, they broke the crock, took out that sponge, wrung out its contents and drank it down.

I suppose it must have happened that way, but I can't help but wonder how that beer tasted!

I Always Tell the Truth (Even if I Have to Lie to Do It) edited by Chris Morley. Greenfield Center, N.Y.: Greenfield Review Press, 1990.

The secret of staying young is to drink good whiskey, eat slowly and lie about your age.

Peter Sejkus walked up to his friend at the bar. "Joe," he said worriedly, "that last drink makes four I've seen you toss down this evening. And you know the doctor told you to drink only one drink a day."

"I know, I know," replied his friend at the bar, pausing to take another drink from his glass. "But I am truly following the doctor's orders. Really I am. Y'see this drink I got here is for September 8, 2005."

The reason Jack never jogs is because it makes the gimlet slosh out of his glass!

Moonshine (whiskey) is known in the hill country of Kentucky, Tennessee, and Arkansas as splo, stump liquor, swamp dew, angel teat, white mule, white lightning, Kentucky fire and squirrel whiskey. Drinking too much "swamp dew" makes a man downsy or gives him the blind billiards.

"Bartender, how much is a shot of whiskey?" the guy asked.

"Two bucks a shot," the bartender replied.

"And how much for a refill?"

"Nothing for the first refill. Two bucks a shot after that."

"Good. Let me have the first refill, please."

Intoxication: Nothing intoxicates some people like a sip of authority. Proof? Ask any buck private in the military!

"I can see that you really like olives, Matilda," Mary Swanson said to her friend.

"Now, I do," her friend replied. "But y'know, Mary, I used to not like 'em at all until a friend showed me how to fix 'em with gin and vermouth."

Cocktail parties: As a rule, more handsome men attend cocktail parties than women because the hostess writes the invitations.

A customer walked into the tavern and sat down at the bar. His dog sat next to him. The bartender said, "Nothin' doin', buster, we don't allow dogs in here."

"But this dog talks. Can't he stay?"

"Aw, c'mon, Mister. No dog can talk!"

"This one can." He turns to the dog and says, "Beetle, what fits on top of a house?"

"Roof!" barked the dog.

"Get outa here, Mister. Any damn dog can say that."

"Okay, okay," the guy says. "Just one more and you'll see. Tell me, Beetle how does sandpaper feel?"

"Ruff!" barks the dog.

"C'mon, that's enough," said the bartender. "Get your ass AND your dog outa here!"

"Let me try him one more time. You'll see. OK?"

"All right. Once more. Then out!"

"Beetle, who was the greatest hitter of all ball players?"

"Ruth!" replies the dog.

"Enough! Out with you now!" the bartender screams.

He picks up both the man and his dog and heaves them out in the gutter.

The dog was the first to recover. He looks questioningly at his master and says, "DiMaggio?"

Drunkenness is a strange egg from which a helluva lot of vices hatch.

TOASTS FOR BREAKFAST

Then fill a fair and honest cup, and bear it straight to
    me;
The goblet hallows all it holds, whate'er the liquid be;
And may the cherubs on its face protect me from the
    sin
That dooms one to those dreadful words,
"My dear, where have you been?"

Holmes

If I should have my choice after I die,
I don't know just where I should wish to go:
For climate I would want to be above
For company — I'd choose to go below.

The hand that rocks the cradle
Is the hand that rules the earth —
But the hand that holds four aces! —
Bet on it for all you're worth.

Here's to the bride that is to be,
Happy and smiling and fair,
And here's to those who would like to be,
And are wondering when, and where.

A man stumbled out of a bar and, walking with his head down, stumbled along the street. As might be expected, he ran headfirst into a lamppost after which he stood swaying from the blow and the whiskey.

A policeman happened by, took the poor guy by the shoulder and asked, "Have an accident, Sir?"

"Much obliged, but no thanks. I just h-h-had one!"

"No doubt alcohol, tobacco, and so forth, are things that a saint must avoid; but sainthood is also a thing that human beings must avoid."

George Orwell

A farm advisor walked into the bar in a small Illinois town. He walked up to the two farmers sitting at the bar and said, "I hear you folks around here have been having trouble with your well-water."

"Yup! That's a fact. We have had trouble," replied one of the farmers. "But we've been using modern techniques and I think we're O.K. now."

"What kind of techniques, if I may ask?" asked the farm advisor.

"For one, we boil the water."

"Good for you."

"Then we filter it."

"Very good idea."

"Then we add the chemical they done give us at the EPA."

"That should do it."

"Then we drink only beer."

He was so drunk that he couldn't hit the ground with his ole hat!

A customer goes to the bar and orders as follows: "Bartender, give me a glass of your very best 12-year-old Scotch."

The bartender was exceedingly busy and had no time to hunt down the aged Scotch, so he grabbed the house bottle, pouring a glass full of it.

The man took just one sip and spat it out. "That is not 12-year-old Scotch! It's only 7-years-old! Please give me what I ordered ... 12-year-old Scotch!"

The fellow really teed-off the bartender who thought he'd try him again, pouring from a bottle of 10-year-old Scotch.

The guy took one sip and handed it back. "This is only 10-years-old, dammit; now give me what I ordered!"

The bartender was really impressed with the guy, never having seen anyone who could so accurately judge the age of whiskey by taste. So he poured him a glass of 8-year-old Scotch.

"I'm getting really mad at you, Bartender. Why do you do this to me? If I wanted 8-year-old Scotch, I'd ask for it. Now bring me what I ordered, a glass of 12-year-old Scotch. And no substitutions this time!"

This time the bartender met the customer's request, pouring him a glass of 12-year-old Scotch. The guy sipped it, smiled and then drank it all. "Thank you, bartender. I'm glad to know you can finally follow an order!"

A drunk at the far end of the bar came staggering up to the customer saying, "I sheen what y-you done, Buddy. I'm impresshed! Here tasht this," he said, handing him his own glass.

The Scotch expert took a drink, spit it out, moaning, "This tastes like piss!"

"I know," said the drunk. "But tell me, h-how old ish it?"

**You've done it again, Marge —
the same thing I had for lunch!**

A guy was attending a convention in Chicago, a few too many drinks and a little spare time, so he went into a tavern, up to the bar and sat down near a pretty woman who was alone. He had a drink or two, then sidled up to the seat next to her and said, "I'm here wish a c-convention but I'd like to b-buy you a d-drink."

She turned jaundiced eyes on him, then said in a nasty tone of voice, "Get away from me, I'm a lesbian."

"Oh yeah?" said the guy. "Howsh things in Beirut?"

"It is a mistake to think that Acerra reeks of yesterday's liquor; Acerra always drinks till next morning."

Martial

A man walked into a bar and sat next to a hot-looking gal.

"How about buying me a drink, Man?" she asked.

After that one, she said, "I'd like another, a double this time."

She downed the drink and asked, "Are you from this town?"

"Yep!" he replied, "a few blocks from here."

"How about doing something with me tonight?" she asked.

"Well, OK, but first I got to know what it'll cost me."

"Fifty bucks for the first hour. Seventy-five for two hours. And for a hundred and fifty, you get the entire night."

"Great," he said, "let's get started."

In his apartment, she peeled off her dress and stood in terribly sensual underthings. "What would you like me to do first?" she asked.

"Please start with the windows," he said.

"Wine is the drink of gods, milk the drink of babies, tea the drink of women, and water the drink of beasts."

Jolen Stuart Blackie — 1809-1915

A Fundamentalist preacher walked into a bar and began to sermonize to those sitting there about the evils of drink. "Let me ask you one question," said the preacher. "If I set a bucket of water and a bucket of whiskey before a donkey, which do you suppose he'd drink?"

A fellow raised his hand. "Yes?" encouraged the preacher.

"The water, of course," said the man at the bar. "What would you expect of a stupid ass!"

'Tis pity wine should be so deleterious,
For tea and coffee leave us much more serious.

Byron

A guy walks into a bar and orders a martini. Finishing it, he ate the olive, then ate the bowl of the glass. But the stem he threw in the trash can.

He noticed that the bartender was looking at him most curiously, so he asked, "You probably think I'm crazy, eh, Bartender?"

"Man, that puts it mildly! The stem's the best part and you threw it away!"

"Never drink from your finger bowl — it contains only water."

Addison Mizner — 1872-1933

He only drinks to calm his nerves
And steadiness improve
Today he got so steady
He couldn't even move.

"Man wants but little here below, but wants that little strong."

Oliver Wendell Holmes — 1809-1894

This guy wandered into a bar and sat down next to an angry-looking man who had several empty shot glasses in front of him. "Hey, Buddy!" the newcomer asked. "You look like last year's tomato. What's happened to you?"

"Well, I tell you ... I had everything in this world a man could want ... a beautiful home and a gorgeous woman to look after it and me, plenty of money and the best car in the world."

"Wow! What happened to you?"
"Well, one day, my wife walked back in."

The Corkscrew: A useful key to unlock the storehouse of wit, the treasury of laughter, the front door of fellowship, and the gate of pleasant folly.

A man walked into the bar at the oldest fine hotel in New York, the Plaza, and ordered a drink. When the bartender served it the man remarked, "You know, I was in here about a year ago, had several drinks and then told you that I couldn't pay for them. You threw me out and broke my leg!"

"Did I? I'm sure sorry about that, Sir," the bartender replied.

"That's all right. I'm recovered now. But I'm going to have to trouble you once again!"

"A soft drink turneth away company."
Oliver Herford — 1863-1935

Two fellows, strangers to one another, met in the bar and hit it off together. One said to the other, "You know, for twenty years my wife and I had a great life. We couldn't have been happier. Then it happened."

"What on earth happened?" asked the other.

"We met."

One time, I told a buddy that my father used to tend bar in a frontier saloon. His comment, and I quote, "Hell, that's nothing! My old man kept one open."

A formidable gent from Taconic
Consumed vodka and rye like a tonic.
But in his ninety-ninth year
He swore off, for fear
(He said) that his thirst might grow chronic.

"We drink to one another's health and spoil our own."

Jerome K. Jerome — 1859-1927

CHANTEY OF NOTORIOUS BIBBERS

Homer was a vinous Greek who loved
the flowing bottle,
Herodotus was a thirsty cuss, and so
was Aristotle.

Chorus

Sing ho! that archipeligo where mighty
Attic thinkers
Invoked the grape to keep in shape,
and lampooned water drinkers.

King Richard fought the heathen Turk,
along with his Crusaders,
On wobbly legs they tippled kegs and
hated lemonaders.

Chorus

Sing ho! the gallant English King, sing
ho! his merry yeomen,
Who felt the need of potent mead to
make them better bowmen.

Bill Shakespeare loved to dip his pen in
Mermaid Inn canary
And Bobby B. was boiled when he
indited "Highland Mary."

Chorus

Sing ho! the buxom barmaid Muse who
did her work on brandy.
She now eschews such vulgar brews and
trains on sugar candy.

Dan Webster stoked his boilers with
brown jugs of apple cider,
And when he made a speech he yanked
the spigot open wider.

Chorus

Sing ho! those spirited debates, bereft
    of all restrictions,
When statesmen carried on their hip
    the strength of their convictions.

Innocent Merriment, An Anthology of Light Verse, by
Franklin P. Adams, Garden City Publishing Co., New York: 1945.

L'Envoi

Now pass the faucet water, lads, and
    pledge in melancholy
The sinful ways of ancient days — for
    alcohol is folly;
Let's live and grow on H-2-0, and shun
    the lethal snicker,
For history is a record of good men
    gone wrong on licker.

Henry Morton Robinson
Men Only, edited by John Henry Johnson
Indianapolis: Maxwell Droke, Pub., 1936

A good cure for a hangover is to drink black coffee the night before instead of the morning after.

Laurence J. Peter

A famous explorer was having a drink at his favorite bar. It was the night before he was to leave on an important expedition and he was telling everybody about the new, proficient equipment he had for his trip.

"Sounds mighty efficient," said a friend at the bar.

"But I've got something here that'll do you a whole lot of good."

"Yeah? What's that?" asked the adventurer.

"Bartender," his friend said, "let me have a small flask of gin, another of vermouth and a tiny shaker. Put 'em on the bar here."

The bartender did that but the explorer said, "You're wasting your time, Friend, because I never drink when I'm on an expedition."

"I hear you," said his friend, "but this trio, in a small case, is an absolute necessity because if you get lost and there's no one around to help you, you just open the case and make a martini. Within minutes, five people will appear in the woods and tell you how you should have mixed it!"

"I've heard him renounce wine a hundred times a day, but then it has been between as many glasses."

Jerrold Douglas — 1803-1857

A gorilla walked into a bar and ordered a martini. Seeing that everyone was staring at him, the gorilla said to the bartender, "Don't worry, man, I'm over twenty-one."

"He drank like a fish, if drinking nothing but water could be so described."

Alfred Edward Housner — 1859-1896

A scarlet monkey, an orange dog, and a pink elephant walked into a bar. They sat down and ordered a round of drinks. The bartender walked up to them and said, "Hey, you guys are a little early. Your man ain't here yet."

Alcoholic: A guy who tries to pull himself out of trouble with a corkscrew.

Ed Baldwin

A big, tough lumberjack, so huge he'd have put Paul Bunyan to shame, walked into a bar and ordered a quadruple martini. "Hey, buddy, where you been all these months?"

"I was working overseas, cutting trees in the Sahara forest."

"Oh. I guess you mean the Sahara desert, don't you?"

"Now, it's a desert!"

"A CLOCK FOR PEOPLE WHO NEVER TAKE A DRINK BEFORE FIVE O'CLOCK? I THINK HE'S GOT SOMETHING THERE, J.B.!"

"Many a man keeps on drinking till he hasn't a coat for either his back or his stomach."

George D. Prentice — 1802-1870

A man walked into a bar and sat down. The bartender came over and asked if he'd like a drink.

"Nope. I tried it once and didn't like it," replied the man.

In a little while, the bartender came back and asked if the man would like a cigar.

"No again, thank you. I tried it once and didn't like it at all."

For the third time the bartender approached the guy, telling him that there was a card game in the next room and asking if the man would like to join the boys.

"No, thank you," the man again replied. "I played once and didn't at all like it. I'll just sit here quietly and wait for my son."

The bartender nodded, stepped back and said, "An only child, I presume."

"It's useless to hold a person to anything he says while he's in love, drunk, or running for office."

Shirley MacLaine

A guy walks into a bar about ten o'clock of a morning, saying, "I never drink before noon, you know, but luckily it's noon in India."

We won't say that Uncle Otto spends a lot of time in the tavern, but his doctor says he's suffering from "bottle fatigue."

THE DYING FISHERMAN'S SONG

'TWAS midnight on the ocean,
Not a street car was in sight;
The sun was shining brightly,
For it had rained all that night.

'Twas a summer's day in winter,
The rain was snowing fast,
As a barefoot girl with shoes on
Stood sitting in the grass.

'Twas evening and the rising sun
Was setting in the west;
And all the fishes in the trees
Were cuddled in their nests.

The rain was pouring down,
The sun was shining bright,
And everything that you could see
Was hidden out of sight.

The organ peeled potatoes,
Lard was rendered by the choir;
When the sexton rang the dishrag
Someone set the church on fire.

"Holy smokes!" the teacher shouted,
As he madly tore his hair.
Now his head resembles heaven,
For there is no parting there.

My Pious Friends and Drinking Companions,
by Frank Shay & John Held, Jr.
New York: Golden Label Books, Inc., 1930.

"Like a camel I can go without a drink for seven days
— and have on several horrible occasions."

Herb Caen

The man walked unsteadily into the bar, appearing quite confused. "Can I help you, Sir?" asked the bartender. "You seem a bit confused."

"Thanks. Maybe you can. I jusht don't unershtand it. I p-put a quarter in the scale out there on the sidewalk and the m-meter shaid that I weighed a-a-an hour!"

He's been thrown out of so many bars, he wears a gray suit so it'll match the sidewalk.

A condemned man, about to be executed, was offered a drink of whiskey just before the gallows was sprung. "Thank you, but no!" he said. "When I drink, I lose all sense of direction!"

"Inflation has gone up over a dollar a quart."

W. C. Fields

A traveling salesman in town for the first time in a year, stopped off for a drink in a bar. He sat beside another man and the two became fast friends. After several hours, the salesman and the man were so fond of one another that they agreed to meet the next year, same time and place.

One year later, the salesman returned to the bar and, sure enough, his friend was sitting there just as he'd promised.

"It's sure good of you to keep our appointment," the salesman said. "I never thought that you'd come back here."

"Who came back!" said the friend. "I never left!"

Abstinence is a noble thing, but it should be practiced in moderation!

A drunk wandering down the street, stops a pedestrian and asks, "Shir ... c-could you t-tell me where I am?"

"You're on the corner of 57th Street and Fifth Avenue."

"Hell, man, I don't need d-details. Jusht tell me what c-city I'm in!"

"I always keep a supply of stimulant handy in case I see a snake. I always keep a supply of snakes handy, too."

W. C. Fields

This guy, terribly disturbed, wandered into the bar and ordered two martinis. When he was served, he gulped them down and ordered two more. When these were served, he gulped them down, too, after which he asked the bartender: "Shay, Mishter bartender, how tall ish a penguin?"

The bartender shaped his hands to fit the size of a penguin and the guy groaned and ordered two more martinis, drank them down and groaned again. "What's the trouble, Mister?" asked the bartender.

"If that's all the taller a penguin ish, den I-I-I've run over a nun!"

––––––––––

"It takes a good deal of courage to ride a horse. This, however, I have. I get it at about fifty cents a flask and take it as required."

Stephen Leacock

––––––––––

A man, already three sheets into the wind, stumbled his way up to the bar, ordered a double scotch and began to talk about world affairs with an old geezer sitting there. Suddenly the old man lurched off of his chair and disappeared for several minutes. Reappearing, his friend, still at the bar, asked where he'd been.

"In the men's room," replied the senior.

"Good idea. Would you go for me?" he said.

Off went the old man who returned quickly to the bar, saying: "You didn't have to go."

**"Whatever you do, don't get into a chug-a-lug contest
with him."**

"It is no time for mirth or laughter. The cold grey dawn
of the morning after."

George Ade

There was an old geezer in a trunk,
Who asked his wife: "Am I drunk?"
She replied with regret:
"You sure are, my pet."
And he answered: "That's just what I thunk."

Ogden Nash

"One drink is just right; two is too many; three are too
few."

Spanish saying

A young man walked into a bar and sat down. Within a few minutes, a very attractive brunette walked in and sat next to him. He was trying to screw up courage to speak to her when suddenly, she sprang to her feet shouting: "The nerve of you! You jerk! I'm not that kind of girl. Meet at your hotel room, you ask? Never!"

The young guy was really put out by this, embarrassed and shocked. So he got up and went to a table where he sat by himself. Soon the girl got up and came over to his table, saying: "Please forgive me, Sir. I was getting material for my doctoral dissertation in psychology, observing reactions all around me. I just wanted to see how you'd react."

"Don't worry about it," said the young man. "Now I'll get yours." He leaped to his feet and yelled at the top of his voice: "Two hundred bucks an hour! Hell, no! No woman is worth that kind of dough!"

"Wine improves with age; the older I get, the more I like it."

Anonymous

A cute, hope-to-be starlet walked into a famous Hollywood bar and ordered a drink. Holding her drink, she wandered around trying to find a face that she knew. At last, she saw a man she recognized, but she wasn't sure. She turned to the bartender and asked, "Say, isn't that Tom Cruise over there?"

"Sure is, Ma'am."

"Well, I'm upset. He keeps annoying me."

"Lady, that's all bunk. He hasn't even looked at you."

"I know. That's what's annoying me."

"Reality is a delusion created by alcohol deficiency."

Anonymous

A lawyer felt nothing but contempt for a particular judge so that, slightly "under the influence," he appeared in court one morning and greeted the judge with: "Howdy, old boy. How's the kid doin' today?" The Judge was furious, saying: "You're drunk!" The lawyer nodded, saying, "That's the first correct judgment I've ever heard Your Honor deliver."

Uncle Josh says that the new tavern in town is the best we've ever had. He says their tables are the best he's ever been under.

Tommy's drinking began in college. Y'see, he graduated Magna Cum Loaded. Why, they tell that his eyes were so red that the Communist Party sent him a membership application.

"I got Mark Hellinger so drunk one night that it took three bellboys to put me to bed."

W. C. Fields

OUT OF THE TAVERN

Out of the tavern I've just stepped tonight,
Street, you are caught in a very bad plight;
Right hand and left hand are both out of place,
Street, you are drunk, it's a very clear case.

Moon, 'tis a very queer figure you cut,
One eye is staring while the other is shut,
Tipsy, I see, and you're greatly to blame,
Old as you are, 'tis a terrible shame.

And now the street lamp — what a scandalous sight,
None of them soberly standing upright,
Rocking and swaggering — why, on my word,
Each of the lamps is as drunk as a lord.

All is confusion — now isn't it odd,
I am the only thing sober abroad;
It would be rash with the crew to remain,
Better go back to the tavern again.

Unknown

"Religions change; beer and wine remain."

Harvey Allen

A guy walked into a bar on 56th Street in New York and sat next to a very attractive woman. After a drink, he said softly to her, "I'd sure like to have you come up to my place."

She sniffed and said, "That'll be the day."

"Would you at least come with me to dinner at the hotel here?"

"That'll be the day!" she hmpfed.

"Well, then, how about coming with me in my jet plane and spending the weekend in Paris and the following week in Southern Italy?"

"This'll be the day."

"The wages of gin is breath."

Studs Lonigan

At the town tavern, Billy Joe is known as a really big gun. You know ... small caliber and immense bore.

The old boozer remarked: "Two drinks are enough for any man, especially if the guy's paid for my first two and I've got to pay for the third!"

Native wit can sometimes be filled with a good measure of wisdom. Consider this from an Ozark hillbilly: "Whiskey is the only cure for snakebite! But it must be used jest right in jest the right way. And, podner, the right way is to hev the whiskey in ya when you is bit."

The physician completed his examination, saying, "I can find nothing wrong that could cause your trouble. I guess the problem is whiskey."

"That's OK, Doc," said the patient. "Maybe you'd better examine me again when you're sober."

The professor of philosophy was taking a walk when he saw an old man sitting in a rocking chair on the porch. He walked up the steps and stood before the old man, saying, "Sir, you appear not to have a care in the world. Amazing! Could you tell me your formula for a long and happy life?"

The old man nodded, cleared his throat and said, "Well, now, lessee. I smoke three packs a day, drink a quart of bourbon daily and four cases of beer a week. I go out each night and never get home till around four o'clock ..."

"Amazing," said the professor. "Just amazing. So tell me, sir, how old are you?"

The old man answers: "Thirty-two!"

"I distrust camels, and anyone else who can go a week without a drink."

Joe E. Lewis

"I'll bet you had a fight with your wife and you're gonna leave me a fifty dollar tip just to spite her!"

This fellow had been spending all day and half the night drinking in a gambling joint. And all of his money had been gambled away. To top it all, he has to go to the restroom but hadn't a dime to his name. So he borrows a dime from a kind gentleman and leaves. But, glory be, there is a stall with the door open! So he saves the dime, finishes in the restroom, returns to the gambling area, puts the dime in a slot machine, hits the jackpot and from that goes on to a chain of winnings that earns him millions of dollars.

He is now famous and starts a lecture tour explaining his formula for success. At each audience, he announces that if he finds the benefactor who saved him that critical dime, he'll give him half his fortune. Then, one night a man in the audience says, "I'm the guy that gave you the dime that started your fortune!"

The lucky gambler yells back, "No! No! It's not the dime; I'm looking for the guy who left that toilet door open."

You're so drunk, your breath gives me a nose bleed.

Bowery philosophy: "Bugs won't never bother a drinkin' man. It's a scientific fact that a muskeeter'll buzz up to a whiskey drinker and take one look or one smell and fly for his life."

"Some men are like musical glasses. To produce their finest tones, you must keep them wet."

Samuel Taylor Coleridge — 1772-1834

Vance Randolph devoted his life to the folklore of Ozark mountain folk. His several books on Ozark lore are not only funny but invaluable historical and philo-sophical records of the ways, thinking, mores of early American hill people. And they were wonderful people: self-reliant, resourceful, fair-minded and decent (with a few exceptions!).

Here is one of Vance Randolph's stories gleaned from hillbilly lore that offers a view of hillbilly life back then. It is from his book — *Stiff as a Poker,* 1955.

THREE BARRELS OF WHISKEY

ONE TIME there was three brothers named Matthew, Mark, and Luke. They helped a moonshiner out of an awful bad mess. If it wasn't for what them three brothers done, that moonshiner would have went to the peniten-tiary, sure. After everything blowed over and settled down, the moonshiner come a-driving into town, and he give Matthew a barrel of good whiskey.

It looks like a barrel of whiskey would last all winter. But Mark and Luke come over to sample the stuff, and pretty soon some of their kinfolks dropped in. All three of them boys was married, so here come a lot of their wife's kinfolks, too. They fetched fried chicken and ham and cake and all kind of victuals. There was a fiddler happened to come along that night, and so they give a big dance. It wasn't no time at all till Matthew's whiskey was plumb gone.

Two or three weeks afterwards the moonshiner come a-driving into town again, and this time he give Mark a barrel of good whiskey. Luke and Matthew come over to sample the stuff, of course, and some of their wife's kinfolks got wind of it. Pretty soon they was having a big jamboree, dancing and drinking and hell-raising just like they done before. It wasn't no time at all till Mark's whiskey was plumb gone.

Two or three weeks after that the moonshiner come a-driving in with a barrel of good whiskey for Luke. This time all the brothers got together, and they figured out a way to keep that whiskey in the family. "Listen, Luke," says Matthew, "soon it gets dark you hide the barrel somewheres. Then tomorrow you can tell them greedy-guts that somebody must have stole it." Mark nodded his head. "All you got to do," he says, "is to tell a straight story and put on a good act." Luke studied about it awhile, and then he says all right.

Soon as it got dark Luke rolled the barrel out in his pasture and piled some brush over it. Matthew and Mark was hid in the woods a-watching him. After Luke went back to the house they siphoned off the whiskey in jugs and buried the jugs in a cave down by the river. Them boys figured it was the best thing to do. They knowed poor Luke couldn't hold out ag'in his wife and her kinfolks.

Next day folks come from all over the country, and they was a-milling around Luke's house like bees round a sorghum mill. He told 'em somebody had stole the whiskey, but they didn't believe it, so finally he give up and went out to the brush pile. When he seen the barrel was empty Luke begun to holler louder'n anybody. "We been robbed!" says he. "The goddam stuff *has* been stole!" Pretty soon the two older brothers come over, and he told 'em what happened.

After while they got him alone for a minute, and Matthew says, "Where did you hide it?" Luke cursed something terrible, and he showed 'em the brush pile and the empty barrel. "You're a-putting on the best act I ever seen, but there ain't no need to keep it up with us," says Mark. "It ain't no act, God damn it!" yells Luke. "The whiskey's gone, I tell you!" His two brothers just looked at him and shook their heads kind of sad. "All right, Luke, if that's the way you want it," says Matthew. So then him and Mark went home and left poor Luke a-hollering and a-quarreling with his wife's kinfolks.

About a week after that Luke found a gallon jug of good whiskey on his porch one morning. A couple weeks later there was another gallon, right in the same place. One time when he had company over Sunday there was two jugs on the porch. Luke had figured the whole thing out by this time, and he knowed in reason where the whiskey come from. But he never said one word about it to anybody. Neither did Matthew and Mark. Them boys was awful close-mouthed about things like that.

Stiff as a Poker — *Joy of Drink,*
Vance Randolph. Barnes & Noble
Publishers. 1993, New York.

If a mosquito bit him, the critter'd die of alcohol poisoning.

Two guys were arguing about the effect of liquor on length of life. "I say that, for sure, if a guy drinks more than 1 1/2 ounces of booze a day, he can take four years off his life."

"That's crazy," said the other guy. "Why, my father drank four martinis every night of his adult life and lived to be 98. And, what's more, he wouldn't have died then if he hadn't come across a couple of rotten olives."

"Whiskey: By far the most popular of all the many remedies that absolutely won't cure a cold."

I like brandy best

Earl Wilson

There is so much drinking today on college campuses that a suggestion of parents of students might just be in order. They suggest that the old saying "Halls of Ivy" be changed to: "The Alco-hols of Ivy!"

Champagne: A beverage which makes you see double but feel single.

Two old drinking buddies were discussing their lives.
"Were you ever in love, George?" one asked.
"Yeah, one time when I was a young guy I did fall in love."
"But you never did get married, did you?"
"Nope," replied George. "Never did. Y'see, the gal wouldn't marry me when I was drunk and I wouldn't marry her when I was sober!"

Reprinted from: *The Wolfpen Notebooks* by James Still
Lexington, Ky.: University Press of Kentucky, 1991

"A drunken night makes a cloudy morning."

Lord Cornwallis

"I had no idea he drank until one day he came home sober."

A socially prominent Chicago woman sent an invitation to a cocktail party that read: "Cocktails 6 to 8."

Her husband thought that it was too unfriendly and that guests would think they must go home at eight. So she changed the invitation to read: "Cocktails at six."

Well, the party came off just fine and everybody was enjoying it so much and seemed reluctant to go home! At one o'clock, the police arrived, saying that a neighbor had complained of the noise. That broke up the party and everybody went home. As the last guest left, the hostess turned to her husband and asked: "I wonder which neighbor complained?"

"It wasn't the neighbor," he said, "I called the cops!"

Alcoholic: One who magnifies his troubles by looking at them through the bottom of a glass!

And here is our famous comedian, WILL ROGERS, commenting on Russian vodka.

Will Rogers was appearing before an audience, and his subject was his recent trip to Russia and his learning about Russian vodka.

"It's made from fermented Russian wheat, corn, oats, barley, alfalfa, or jimsonweed, just which ever one of these they happen to have handy. Then they start adding the ingredients."

"Potato peelings is one of 'em, then Russian boot tops. You just take the tops of as many Russian boots as you can get when the men are asleep, you harvest 'em just above the ankle."

"The next ingredient (the Russians always deny this to me, but I have always believed it's true) is the whiskers. They say that they don't put 'em in vodka, that they are only used in that soup called borsch."

"Finally it's fermented and the Russian vodka is ready to drink."

"When you do your eyes begin expanding, and your ears begin to flop like a mule's. It's the only drink where you drink and try to grit your teeth at the same time. It gives the most immediate results of any libation ever concocted, you don't have to wait for it to act. By the time it reaches the Adams apple it has acted. A man stepping on a red-hot poker could show no more immediate animation. It's the only drink where you can hit the man that handed it to you before he can possibly get away."

"It's a timesaver. It should especially appeal to Americans, there is nothing so dull in American life as that period when a drinker is at that annoying stage. He is a pest to everybody, but vodka eliminates that, you are never at the pest period."

Will Rogers was arguing about the effects of alcohol, with Will taking the affirmative side. Here's his argument: "The wine had such ill effects on Noah's health that it was all he could do to live 950 years. Just nineteen years short of Methusaleh," remarked Will. "Show me a total abstainer that ever lived that long!"

WHEN I DIE

When I die, don't bury me at all,
Just pickle my bones in alcohol:
A scuttle of booze
At my head and shoes,
And then my bones will surely keep.

ONE MORE DRINK FOR THE FOUR OF US

I was drunk last night,
Drunk the night before;
Going to get drunk tonight
If I never get drunk any more.

'Cause when I'm drunk
I'm as happy as can be:
For I am a member
Of the souse familee.

Glorious, glorious,
One more drink for the four of us.
Sing glory be to hob there's no more of us
For one of us could kill it all alone.

My Pious Friends and Drunken Companions
by Frank Shay & John Held, Jr.
New York: Gold Label Books, Inc., 1930

A bumper of good liquor
Will end a contest quicker
Than justice, judge, or vicar.

Sheridan

The battleship had been gone for eight months in the South Pacific so that when it returned stateside, the crew was ready for a refreshing liberty. Everything went well until one sailor showed up carrying two bottles of whiskey. He staggered up the gangway but was stopped by the officer on duty who was amused to see the guy and said, "Sailor, you are not allowed to bring liquor aboard ship. So I'm going to turn my back and I want to hear two splashes in the water. Then you can come aboard and we'll forget the matter."

The officer turned around, heard two splashes and was satisfied. But he was startled to see the sailor, still with a bottle in each hand, lurching quickly out of sight ... in his stocking feet!

No man shall be held as mellow
Who can distinguish blue from yellow.

He'd been with the boys until far too late that night. It was almost 4 A.M.! And he'd promised to be home by 11 P.M. That night at his door, he managed to get his key into the lock, open the door and tip-toe in. As he reached the stairs, the clock began to cuckoo four times. Then the idea came to him and when the clock quit at four cuckoos, he imitated it and cuckooed seven times, thinking that'll fool her. He undressed on the stairs, crept up them and into the bedroom, got into bed and she never stirred. Victory!

At breakfast next morning, his wife said: "Amos, we're going to have to do something about that cuckoo clock. It's gone wacky. Last night, as I was laying in bed waiting for you, it cuckooed four times, then it hiccupped then it said, 'damn' and then it cuckooed seven more times. We got to get it fixed!"

Heard at a cocktail party: "I don't mind the smell of liquor near as much as I do listening to it."

A tourist was sitting at the bar in a hotel in Capetown, South Africa. Suddenly, he noticed on the stool beside him, a tiny figure dressed immaculately in a military uniform. That figure was not more than six inches tall! The bartender noticed his interests and said, "Sir, I want you to meet Major Downbeat." The tourist nodded.

"Major, tell this gentleman about the time you called that bloody witch doctor a damned fool!"

Drunk: "Say, Mister, how about a buck for a poor guy?"

Pedestrian: "Heck no! If you'd asked me for a quarter or even half a buck, maybe I'd give it to you. But a buck?"

Drunk: "Enough! Gimme a buck or no ... that's up to you. But don't try to tell me how to run my business!"

Shorty didn't know whether to feed or starve himself so he drowned it.

Two guys were sitting at the bar when one of them pointed at the row of bottles standing behind the bar. "See that, Fred? Vat 69. Astonishing!"

"Why, it's only a bottle of booze! What's astonishing about that?"

"Well, y'see ... I always thought Vat 69 was the Pope's telephone number."

He who drinks one glass a day,
Will live to die some other way.

Stanlicus

Pure water is the choicest gift
    That man to man can bring.
But who am I that I should want
    The best of everything?

Let princess revel with the tap
    Kings with the pump make free;
Whisky, wine or even beer
    Is good enough for me.

What's drinking?
A mere pause from thinking.

Byron

Don't buy a fifth on the third for the Fourth because he who drives forth with a fifth on the Fourth may never drive forth on the fifth.

Pun-American Newsletter, Deerfield, IL

If you'd know when you've enough
Of the punch and the claret cup,
It's time to quit the blessed stuff
When you fall down and can't get up.

Two drunks were having a ball at a cocktail party when one of them said to the other: "I think you've had more than enough to drink, Buddy. Your face is already getting blurred."

In the crowded bus, a guy from Atlanta, Georgia sat opposite a pretty young lady wearing a very short skirt. She was continually trying to tug and pull and stretch the skirt down to her knees but it always crept right back up. At last the Atlanta guy said, "Don't have a hissie, Sis, mah weakness is bourbon."

The good old boy had made a night of it and awakened the next day with a head in proportion to the quantity of drinks the night before. He suffered with ... what else ... The Wrath of Grapes.

Water wagon: A vehicle from which a man frequently dismounts to boast of the fine ride he's having.

Did you hear about the alcoholic who read the sign saying: "Drink Canada Dry," so he went there and tried to do it.

A tavern habitue was given a piano for Christmas. This is how he described his pleasure at receiving it: "It sure has given me a lot of pleasure. Y'see, I sold it and bought whiskey!"

To be bowed by grief is folly;
Naught is gained by melancholy;
Better than the pain of thinking,
Is to steep the sense in drinking.

Alcaeus

The Seven Stages of Inebriety (You got it ... drunk!)
1. Happy
2. Tight
3. Drunk
4. Squiffy
5. Binged
6. Stinko
7. Blotto

Problem drinker: One who never buys.

I have known many,
Liked a few,
Loved one —
Here's to you!

Here's to luck, and hoping God will take a likin' to us!

Cowboy, Dakota

Here's to those who wish us well,
And those who don't, may go to — Heaven.

James Keene

Here's to a kiss:
Give me a kiss, and to that kiss add a score,
Then to that twenty add a hundred more;
A thousand to that hundred, and so kiss on,
To make that thousand quite a million.
Treble that million, and when that is done
Let's kiss afresh as though we'd just begun.

Here's to the love that lies in woman's eyes,
And lies, and lies, and lies.

Here's to you two and to we two,
If you two love we two
As we two love you two,
Then here's to we four!
But if you two don't love we two
As we two love you two,
Then here's to we two and no more.

Drunker than a lord, the guy carried his suitcase into the parked and ready inner-city bus. He stumbled down the aisle, finally sprawling in the lap of an elderly lady who was seated and waiting for the bus to start.

"You drunken bum!" the old lady said. "You're heading straight for hell!"

"Holy samoleans," the drunk groaned, "I'm on the w-wrong b-b-bus!"

Drinking doesn't drown your sorrows ... it merely irrigates them.

When your companions get drunk and fight, take up your hat and wish them goodnight.

He swaggered into the bar, big, burly and nasty as he cased the joint. His eyes fell on a drunk passed out on the floor. He looked at the dead drunk guy and said, "Gimme a double shot of that!"

Never drink on an empty wallet.

A big lug of a guy walks into the bar and yells, "Ain't nobody in these parts I can't whip! I aim to gouge out the eyes of anyone cares to doubt me. I eat barb wire for breakfast, TNT for lunch and live rattlesnakes for my supper. I can dig a mile-long trench, six feet deep in one hour and I can beat the hell out of every man in a city of ten thousand!"

Just then a guy sitting at the end of the bar comes over and hits the loud mouth in the belly and chin, bowling him over. The braggert raises his head and says: "Who the hell are you?"

"I'm the hombre you thought you were when you shot off your big mouth!"

Teetot'lers die the same as others,
So what's the use of knocking off the beer?

A. P. Herbert

The tavern bouncer had already thrown the same guy out of the place six times but he kept coming back. A fellow who was drinking at the bar, says: "Hey, buddy, you're puttin' too much backspin on him!"

I knew this cute gal who had only one thing wrong with her ... she thought she was the cream of society. And, y'know, whenever I took her out she did spend the evening at the top of a bottle.

My boss had to quit his beloved three-martini lunches. The trouble was ... those lunches were cutting into his cocktail hour.

Not drunk is he who from the floor
Can rise alone and still drink more;
But drunk is he, who prostrate lies,
Without the power to drink or rise.

T. L. Peacock

ROWDY BAR

"OH, YEAH? MY ANCESTORS CAME OVER ON THE A_PRILFLOWER!_"

Yes, theirs was a love that was tidal
And it ended in cheer that was bridal.
But the bridegroom said, "Dear,
Let us please have some beer,"
And they buried them seidel by seidel.

Bartender's guide: A stirring account.

At a bistro, a chap named O'Reilly
Said, "I've heard these martinis praised heilly,
But they're better by far
At the neighboring bar
Where they're mixed much more smoothly and dreilly."

Hard Drinking: The easiest thing some men do.

A rheumatic old man from White Plains
Who will never stay in when it rains.
Has a home full of gin
Kept in a great big, wide bin.
That's all he gets for his pains.

The cocktail party is easily the worst invention since
Castor Oil.

Elsa Maxwell

Well, if it's a sin to like Guinness,
Then that I admits what my sin is.
I like it with fizz,
Or just as it is,
And it's much better for me than gin is.

Cyril Ray

A scion of Boston society
Was pinched, and for mere insobriety.
"I will lay in the gutter,
Refusing to utter
One work in defence of sobriety."

Conrad Aiken

A truly modern cowboy story would have the cowhand ride his horse up to the bar, but then the poor guy wouldn't find a place to park his horse.

Back in the 1830's, our frontiersmen, like Davy Crockett, were some punkins when it came to big talk, brags and tall tales. Here is Davy Crockett addressing the U.S. Congress. This is his actual speech. Americans were red-blooded men back in those days — 1837 A.D. Of course, Davy was an inventive humorist and the Congressmen knew that.

CONGRESSMAN CROCKETT'S WELL-SOAKED SPEECH

"Mr. Speaker:

Who — Who — Whoop — Bow — Wow — Wow — Yough. I say, Mr. Speaker; I've had a speech in soak this six months, and it has swelled me like a drowned horse; if I don't deliver it I shall burst and smash the windows. The gentleman from Massachusetts (Mr. Everett) talks of summing up the merits of the question, but I'll sum up my own. In one word I'm a screamer, and have got the roughest racking horse, the prettiest sister, the surest rifle and the ugliest dog in the district. I'm a leetle the savagest crittur you ever *did see*. My father can whip any man in Kentucky, and I can lick my father. I can out-speak any man on this floor, and give him two hours start. I can run faster, dive deeper, stay longer under, and come out drier, than any *chap* this side the big *Swamp*. I can outlook a panther and outstare a flash of lightning, tote a steamboat on my back and play at rough and tumble with a lion, and an occasional kick from a *zebra*. To sum up all in one word *I'm a horse*. Goliah was a pretty hard colt but I could choke him. I can take the rag off — frighten the old folks — astonish the natives — and beat the Dutch all to smash — make nothing of sleeping under a blanket of snow — and don't mind being frozen more than a rotten apple.

"Congress allows *lemonade* to the members and has it charged under the head of stationery — I move also that *whiskey* be allowed under the item of *fuel.* For *bitters* I can suck away at a noggin of aquafortis, sweetened with brimstone, stirred with a lightning rod, and skimmed with a hurricane. I've soaked my head and shoulders in Salt River, so much that I'm always corned. I can walk like an ox, run like a fox, swim like an eel, yell like an Indian, fight like a devil, spout like an earthquake, make love like a mad bull, and swallow a Mexican whole without choking if you butter his head and pin his ears back."

From *Davy Crockett's Almanac, of Wild Sports in the West, Life in the Backwoods, & Sketches of Texas,* Vol. I, No. 3, 1837, p. 40. Nashville, Tennessee: Published by the heirs of Col. Crockett.

Husband: "Dear, drinking makes you beautiful."
Wife: "But I haven't had even one drink."
Husband: "I know, but I've had several."

WCTU zealot: "Sir! Don't you know that whiskey is slow poison?"
Drinker: "I sure do, Sister, but I ain't in no hurry!"

Barroom sign: The Customer Is Always Tight!

Did you hear about the careless guy who dropped a few drops of whiskey from his glass into the goldfish bowl? Well, those goldfish flipped out of the bowl and chased his cat down the street!

Whiskey: A great drink if you don't weaken — it.

The bartender spotted a customer sitting at the bar with his napkin tucked into his collar. The bartender motioned a waiter over and told him to ask the customer to remove the napkin and stop displaying such bad manners. The waiter thought a bit, then walked to the customer and diplomatically asked: "Shave or haircut, Sir?"

"Ma'am, I'm your new neighbor and I need a bottle opener. Do you have one?"

"Sorry. He's gone to work."

Husband: "Dear, we had a drinking contest at the club today."

Wife: "Really! And who won second prize?"

The surest way to lose your health is to continue drinking to other people's!

Bartender: "I run the toughest, fightenest, wranglest bar in town!"

Customer: "I don't think you're so tough. I never seen cleaner sawdust on the floor of a bar!"

Bartender: "That ain't sawdust ... it's what's left of the furniture from last night!"

Champagne: made of three dollars' worth of wine and three dollars' worth of bubbles.

He's the heaviest drinker in town. Why, the mosquitoes have to take along a glass of water before they sting him. How come? They can't take his blood without a chaser.

Here's some excellent advice for alcoholics, the chronic kind, given years ago when a buck was a buck. But if you figure the changed value of the dollar, you can see that this bit of advice offers the perennial drinker an alternative to mere drinking at the bar with the boys.

Here is a piece of well-thought-out advice for chronic alcoholics: Since you cannot refrain from drinking, why not open your own bar in your own home? It's very easy. Being the only customer, you won't need a license. Just give your wife $55 to buy a case of whiskey. There are 240 shots to a case. Buy all of your drinks from your wife at 60¢ a shot. In two weeks, when the case is used up, your wife will have $89 to put in the bank, and $55 to go in business all over again. Now, if you live ten years, and continue to buy all your liquor from your wife, and then get trampled to death by pink elephants, your widow will have over $27,000 on deposit, enough for your funeral, enough to send the children through school [high school!], pay off the mortgage, marry a decent man, and forget she ever knew you!

**"I'm limiting myself to just 2 drinks a day ...
at the present I'm 26 weeks ahead."**

I never could understand how that gal could drink so much whiskey! She could drink twice as much as a man ... and then some! Well, I discovered how that could be when I read in an arithmetic book that one gal is equal to four quarts!

"I'd take a bromo only I can't stand the noise."

Joe E. Lewis

"What do you think I should drink tonight, Henry?" the customer asked the bartender.

"Why not try my rum flip? It's very good for you, has sugar, milk and rum. The sugar gives you plenty of energy. The milk gives you strength."

"But what about the rum?"

"The rum gives you ideas about what to do with all that energy and strength!"

It is true that whiskey won't cure a cold ... but it fails in the most delightful, agreeable, absolutely pleasant way.

I go to the O.K. Saloon because they take such considerate care of me. Why, when I pass out, they take me outside and lay me tenderly alongside the curb. It's the only place I go where I get really good curb service!

For a bad hangover, take the juice of two quarts of whiskey.

Old Sam Jones is an absolutely unredeemed drunk! I watched him breathe on the back of a brunette's neck and he bleached her hair blonde!

A glass is good, and a lass is good,
And a pipe to smoke in cold weather,
The world is good and people are good,
And we're all good fellows together.
Let schoolmasters puzzle their brains
with grammar and nonsense and learning,
Good liquor, I stoutly maintain,
Gives genius a better discerning.

Here's to man; — he is like a kerosene lamp; he is not especially bright; he is often turned down; he generally smokes; and he frequently goes out at night.

A guest in a hotel has had too many drinks. He leaves his room, goes down the hall and enters the hotel elevator. It stops on the way down. A woman, completely naked, gets on the elevator. The drunk guy stares and stares and finally says, "M-my wife's got an outfit shust like yours."

The saloon-keeper loves a drunk — but not as a son-in-law.

Moe and Pete walked into a bar and Moe ordered three whiskey sours. He drank them in one gulp! Then he stepped back, staggered around and fell flat on his face. Pete turned to the bartender and said, "That's Moe for you. One helluva of a guy. He knows exactly when he's had enough!"

The three most fatal diseases in the West are: smallpox, cholera, and the ignorance to argue with a long-haired whiskey-drinkin' liar.

They say that "Love makes the world go 'round." While that may be true, take it from me that whiskey'll do the same thing and it's a cheaper way to go.

We always say: "Take it easy" while layin' one on. Why? Because sweat is a waste of whiskey.

The big, tough he-man type was asked what he did all day. "I hunt and I drink," he replied.

"Yeah? Well, what do you hunt?"

"Something to drink."

A good drinking buddy never heard the story before.

Parson Johnson, the minister of the Ecumenical Church of Peter, was his usual fiery self while preaching on the terrible state of sin in the congregation. He paused after going well into his sermon and asked, "If this congregation has sinners, will they please stand!" Only one person stood ... an old lady named Mary Rose.

"Mary Rose!" said the preacher showing his surprise. "You? Guilty of sin?"

"Oh, excuse me, Parson Johnson. I thought you said *gin*!"

Driving him from a big party, George's wife, Amy, remarked, "Well, George, I must say that you made an ass of yourself tonight. I ... just ... pray that nobody realized you were sober."

If you wake up feelin' halfway between "Oh, Lord" and "My God!" you overdid it.

TOASTS FOR LUNCH

I've drunk your health in company,
I've drunk your health alone.
I've drunk your health so many times,
I've damn near ruint my own.

God made man, frail as a bubble;
Man made love — love made trouble.
God made the vine, —
Then, is it a sin
That man made wine
To drown trouble in?

Let us have wine and women, mirth and laughter —
Sermons and soda-water the day after.

Byron

A Frenchman drinks his native wine,
A German drinks his beer;
An Englishman his 'alf and 'alf,
Because it brings good cheer;
The Scotchman drinks his whiskey straight,
Because it brings on dizziness;
An American has no choice at all, —
He drinks the whole damned business.

A drunken tongue tells what's on a sober mind.

Drinking: What a man does to forget, but the only
thing he forgets is when to stop.

It had been a long, troublesome delivery, the pressure
of which caused husband Donald to drink far more than
he should have! But the ordeal finally ended and the
obstetrician informed him that he had been granted
twins! "Thash jusht fine, Doc. But don't t-tell m'wife. I
want to shurprise h-her."

Age gentles men and whiskey.

A nutty old boozer named Sleaze,
Thought his home was infested with fleas.
So he used gasoline,
Well, his form was last seen,
Rising over the tops of the trees.

The bartender was bored listening to all the great, unusual successes of the man at the bar. "I'm impressed, I must say," interrupted the bartender. "But, Sir, can you tell me anything that you can't do?"

"Well, there's one thing. Ahem! I can't pay your bill."

Jerry Simola is so hen-pecked at home that when he opens a bottle of beer, it doesn't go "Pop!" but "Mom!"

"George! What the heck are you doing out this late at night?"

"Going home from a New Year's party."

"What? Why this is July. New Year's was months ago!"

"I know, I just thought it was about time to go home."

I had a really good time at the party last night. But the bad thing was that I nearly caught cold with such a thin table over me!

"What'll you have to drink, Sir?"

"Water'll be fine."

"Later. You can wash up later. What'll you have to drink?"

There's a guy in Decatur, Illinois who gets pickled so often, they call him "Cucumber!"

"I'm Jerome and I'll be your waiter."

The thoroughly soused guy staggered into the drug store and asked, "Shay, Mishter. You got anything fer a shplittin' headache?"

The druggist sold him an ice bag. But a few hours later, the guy staggers back into the store, walked up to the clerk and says, "I need a l-larger size. I been tryin' fer two hoursh t'git my head inshide this damn thing."

It's less painful to be dead drunk than dead hungry.

John Barrymore, the actor, was being instructed on his performance in a new play on Broadway. "Now," said the director, "in this play as the curtain opens you are in the process of drinking yourself to death."

Barrymore interrupted him: "Can I begin rehearsals now?"

Old Man: "Sailor, I got to tell you that when I was in the Navy, and I was in for five years, I had a great old time."

Young Ensign: "Good to hear that, Sir. What was your capacity?"

Old Man: "Two quarts a day!"

A smile from a good woman is worth more'n a dozen handed out by a bartender.

Mike Flynn had far too much to drink. Finally, he staggered out of the bar only to crash into a light post. Reeling and rubbing his head, he moved away only to fall over the fire hydrant. Back from that impact, he backed into a basement stairwell, landing in a bloody mess. That did it. He curled up and said, "To hell with all this damned traffic, I'll shusht shnuggle up here til the p-parade pashes."

Down in the hill country of Arkansas, young Bill Heffernan thought he'd best speak to his grandfather about the old man's increasing deafness. So he did, after making an appointment with a hearing specialist in Little Rock and talking the old man into seeing him.

When the old guy returned, Bill hurried to his house and asked: "Well, Grandpa, how y'all doin' now ya done seen thet thar hearin' man?"

"Tell ya what, son," the old man replied. "He done fixed me up real good. Sold me a hearin' thang that cost five hundred bucks. But I ain't agonna war the derned thang."

"Why not Grandpa?"

"Well, the doctuh done asked me if I was a drinkin' man and I told him I drunk nigh onto two quarts a day.

He done told me I had to quit drinkin' or the hearin' aid wouldn't do me no good. So I says to him, 'Doc, I like drinkin' so much better'n what I been hearin' lately that I'll jist keep right on gittin deaf!'"

Morning-after questions: "How many men did I whip?"
"Did anyone get killed?"
"Is there something wrong with my eyes?"
and "Whose boots am I wearing?"

A worker at the local brewery had fallen into a huge vat of beer and drowned. At the funeral home, two of his working buddies stood beside the casket and one remarked sadly: "The poor guy never had a chance, did he?"

"Oh, I don't know about that," said the other man, "he got out twice to go to the bathroom."

There is an ancient Jewish story about how Noah helped restore the earth after the flood. It seems that he wanted to restore a vineyard so he joined with Satan to do just that. Satan killed a lamb and let the blood sink into the soil. Then he killed a lion, a monkey and a pig and spread the blood from each of them across the entire vineyard.

You might ask how we know all this and here is how and why we know: When you drink a little, you feel sleepy as a lamb. When you drink a little more, you feel fearless as a lion. And if you take on still more, you begin to hop around like a monkey. Now! If you take on even more drink, and keep on and on at it, well, you become as disgusting as a pig.

James Truslow Adams told a story about two sailors reliving their past while they sat drinking in an old-fashioned bar, complete with old-fashioned fixtures. "I really don't mind these modern bar fixtures so much; it's what they don't have — like spittoons — that I miss."

"But you always did," his buddy replied.

If it takes liquor to build your courage, you might have to prove it.

FIVE REASONS

If on my theme I rightly think,
There are five reasons why I drink,
Good wine, a friend, because I'm dry,
Or lest I should be by and by
Or any other reason why.

Reprinted from *Rowdy Rhymes*
Peter Pauper Press, 1952

My Uncle Louis has to take a drink sometimes, just to steady his nerves. And y'know what? There are times when he gets so steady he can't move!

BEST FRUIT CAKE EVER

1 cup butter	1 tsp. salt
1 cup sugar	lemon juice
4 large eggs	1 cup brown sugar
1 cup dried fruit	nuts
1 tsp. soda	1 or 2 quarts whiskey

Before you start, sample the whiskey to check for quality.

Good isn't it? Now go ahead. Select a large mixing bowl, measuring cup, etc. Check the whiskey again as it must be just right. To be sure the whiskey is of the highest quality, pour one level cup into a glass and drink it as fast as you can. Repeat. With an electric mixer beat 1 cup of butter in the large fluffy bowl. Add 1 tsp of thugar and beat again. Meanwh-i-le, make sure that the whiskey is of the finest quality. Cry another cup. Open 2nd quart if necessary. Add 2 arge leggs, 2 cups of fried druit and beat till high. If druit gets stuck in beaters, just pry it loose with drewscriver. Sample the whiskey again, thecking for tonsicisity. Then sift 2 cups of salt or any-thing, it realy doesn't matter. SAMPLE THE WHISKEY. Sift 2 pint lemon juice, fold in chopped butter and strained nuts. Add 1 babblespoon of brown thugar, or whatever color you can find and wix mell. Grease oven and turn cake pan to 350 degrees. Now pour the whole mess into coven and ake. Check the whiskey again, and again. An'... an'... might good!

Reprinted with permission from: *Grandma's Little Books*,
Dorothy Galyean, Springdate, UT.

Back in those awful days of Prohibition, a cop stopped a car driven by a bootlegger suspect. He examined the car and, low and behold, the floor was covered with filled fruit jars.

"What's in them jars, Mister?" the cop asked.

"The Lord's purest production ... water," said the driver.

The cop removed one lid and sipped the contents ... "Water!" screamed the cop. "That sure as hell don't taste like water to me. It's whiskey!"

"Lordy, lordy, lordy," moaned the driver. "Jesus has done it again!"

Whiskey: Trouble arranged in liquid form.

They drove toward the city in a zig-zag pattern. But suddenly, George, one of the two guys in the car, asked:

"Ish we near Rochester yet? Seems like we're hittin' more people, so I guessh we're gettin' close. Think you oughta be drivin' shlower?"

"Whadaya mean, 'drivin' slower!' You're drivin'."

Gordon was struggling to open his apartment door with his key, but his swaying side-to-side made it difficult. A friend happened by, saw the problem and said, "Here, Gordon, let me help you with that key."

"Ain't neccesshary," Gordon assured him. "But it'd help if you'd hold the house shteady!"

The guy was lit mighty fine when he staggered up to a machine, put in 50¢, pressed a lever and took a sandwich that popped out. He put another coin in and got another sandwich. On and on he went, depositing 50¢ and getting a variety of sandwiches.

A guard noticed the drunken man and went up to him, saying, "That's enough, Mister. Why don't you quit and go home."

"What?" the drunk shrieked, "Just when I'm on a winnin' streak?"

"Yes, your estimate is ready, we were just celebrating it!"

It is certainly odd that you add whiskey to make it strong, and water in the whiskey to make it weak, then lemon to sour it and sugar to sweeten it. Why, a man could get cockeyed just thinkin' about it.

_____

Polishin' your boots on a brass rail is dangerous to your wealth.

_____

MORE AND MORE LIMERICKS

If you feel that you're right on your beam ends,
If your gait is more rolling than seamen's,
And if camels in helmets
March over the pelmets.
You've a touch of delirium tremens.

Leslie Johnson

"Here's to abstinence. May we always practice it in moderation."

Anonymous

An epicure, dining at Crewe,
Found a rather large mouse in his stew;
Said the waiter: "Don't shout, Or wave it about,
Or the rest will be wanting one too."

Anonymous

One of the most interesting and devastating periods in American life was between 1920 and 1933 when the 18th Amendment served to prohibit the free manufacture and sale of liquor. This period produced the class known as bootleggers, of whom the most famous was Al Capone. But many unknown citizens made a living from the illegal manufacture and sale of booze/or "moonshine." A plethora of tales arose around the illegal activities of these small-time producers of illegal moonshine. We print a few of these tales just as they were printed in the book: *Joe Creason's Kentucky*, made up of articles he wrote and published in the *Courier Journal* and the *Louisville Times* of Louisville, Kentucky, the state that got the most notoriety from the illegal activity of distilling whiskey.

Here are a few of Joe Creason's stories about these colorful, often illiterate characters who furnished illicit whiskey to thirsty Americans during the trying period of Prohibition.

"And just what kind of elixir is this moonshine, this white lightning that's been made for so long and remains so illegal?" Joe Creason was asked and replied: "For those who never sampled it, perhaps a description by Irvin S. Cobb, the Kentucky humorist, will suffice."

"It smells," Mr. Cobb wrote, "like gangrene starting in a mildewed silo; it tastes like the wrath to come; and when you absorb a deep swig of it you have all the sensations of having swallowed a lighted kerosene lamp. A sudden jolt of it has been known to stop a victim's watch, snap both of his suspenders, and crack his glass eye right across — all in the same motion."

There was a time when it was a dead-serious game the moonshiners played with the revenuers. Shootings in the old days were common. Now gunplay is infrequent. The agents treat the moonshiner with firm respect and he repays in kind.

As you might suspect, the typical moonshiner isn't much on books and such. A story is told about an old gent named Joshua who was brought before Federal Judge H. Church Ford, a great Bible student.

"So your name is Joshua," Judge Ford mused. "Are you the Joshua who made the sun stand still?"

"No, sir, Judge," came the answer. "I'm the Joshua who made the moonshine still!"

But despite his shortcomings in formal education, the moonshiner usually has the native intelligence and cunning of a fox. This he shows in the cat and mouse game he plays with the revenuers.

Some moonshiners are craftsmen of a sort who take a left-handed kind of pride in their produce. Like the man who was seized at a Monroe County still. While they were wrecking his still, the agents filled a jar with whisky, explaining it would be sent to a lab for analysis.

"Fellers," said the moonshiner seriously, "have that man at the laboratory test it keerful and if he finds anything wrong to let me know 'cause I've always made the best 'shine in this country and I don't want to lose my reputation!"

As proof (100 proof, of course) of how foxy a moonshiner or a bootlegger can be, there's the story of the out-of-town prohibition agent who was imported into a

Western Kentucky town to lay a trap for a man suspected of being a peddler.

Shortly after arriving, the agent spotted the suspect standing on a street corner. Apparently he'd been shopping since he was carrying a shoe box under his arm.

"Could you tell me where a man could buy a pint of whisky in this town?" the under cover man whispered, sidling up to him.

"Gimme two dollars and hold these shoes for me," the suspected bootlegger said, handing him the box, "and I'll see what I can do for you."

The agent did as instructed. The suspect disappeared. An hour passed and the agent stood, patiently holding the box, waiting for the man to return. After two hours he began to smell a king-sized mouse and he opened the box.

Sure enough, there was his pint of whisky!

Drinking: They who can stand drinking usually drink standing.

Some of the favorite tales told by Clay Wade Bailey, the Frankfort newsman, concern moonshine trials heard in the federal court presided over by the late A. M. J. Cochran.

During Prohibition, he recalls, several men were tried at one time in a case; all were found guilty and the judge doled out rather stiff sentences for all hands.

"You know," Bailey heard a relative of one of the moonshiners say as he left the courtroom, "that judge shore is generous with other people's time, ain't he?"

Years ago a bunch of the boys in the Short Creek section of Grayson County set out to drink all the moonshine around. When one of the men passed out cold, the other revelers deposited him among the tombstones in Silain Cemetery and went on with their carousing.

They returned to him early the next morning just as he was prying open his blood shot eyes and viewing his surroundings.

"I'll be damned," they heard him mutter in a semi-stupor, "resurrection mornin' and I'm the first one up!"

Some years back, inadvertently, I started a novice on his way to a moonshining career that ended in prison almost before it had begun.

After going on a raid with federal agents, I wrote a story for *The Courier-Journal Magazine* which included a rather precise recipe for moonshine. A few weeks later a man was arrested in Shively on a moonshine charge. When he was brought to court, Federal Judge Roy M. Shelbourne asked where he'd learned to make the stuff.

"I read it in *The Courier-Journal Magazine*," the man confessed.

"Well," the judge concluded as he sentenced the man to a vacation in Atlanta, "from now on I advise you to stick to the comic pages!"

They say a hangover from over-indulging in moonshine is one of the most severe head-throbbers that can be inflicted on mortal man. Many are the remedies that have been prescribed to counter it, one of the most unusual being the antidote passed on to R. B. Campbell, a Hyden banker, by a notorious moonshine quaffer who lived on Trace Branch in Leslie County.

"The only way to keep from feelin' bad after gettin' drunk on moonshine," he reasoned, "is to get drunk again the next day!"

William Short, an aide to Lieutenant Governor Julian Carroll, comes from Casey County and, like most natives of that area, he has more stories than Boston has beans.

One yarn concerns a young farm boy who had such a drinking problem that he kept all the local moonshiners working overtime just keeping up with his consumption. Since his parents knew of his habit, he had to hide his liquor all over the place — in the straw stack, the corn crib, anywhere.

This day his father was working on the barn when in a stall he found a whisky bottle which, ironically, didn't contain booze but brake fluid the boy had drained into it. The father uncorked the bottle and took a deep swig.

"Gad," he sputtered almost gagging, "no wonder this stuff's a-killin' poor Fred!"

In western Kentucky, some years back, a new cafe in a dry county was raided the very first week it opened and the proprietor was charged with bootlegging whisky. The next day some of the local citizens, including one unfortunate who wasn't exactly the smartest guy around, were talking about how surprised they were by the development.

"I didn't know he was bootleggin'," remarked this poor unfortunate, "but I knowed he was servin' an awful good Coke in there!"

"A snifter of brandy with a male chaser please."

It was in Paducah I heard the story of a man who repeatedly was hauled into court for being drunk in public from indulging well if not wisely in moonshine. Finally, the judge got tired of seeing him so often and called him into his chambers for a stern lecture.

"Have you ever thought of giving up drinking this rot gut and trying Alcoholics Anonymous?" the judge asked.

"No, Judge," the drunk replied, "but I doubt I could afford any of them expensive brands!"

Robert Bolds, who now lives in Louisville, came from a section along the Ohio River in Daviess County known as Tiwoppity Bottom. The area is called that because of the "tiwoppity, tiwoppity" sound made by waves when they slap against the bottom of an old-fashioned johnboat.

Some years back, Bolds claims, the local Catholic priest met one of his parishioners, a man noted for his intemperate habits. Since the man was in his cups even then, the priest was revolted by the sight.

"Drunk again!" the priest fussed.

"Me, too Father," the drunk lisped, "me, too!"

A man was nabbed by the feds at his still in eastern Kentucky for the ninth time. When he came up for trial, he was found guilty and ordered to stand before the judge for sentencing.

"You know," the judge said, "this is getting to be something of a habit, your appearing before me like this. Before passing sentence on you, I just want you to know that you have given this court more trouble than anyone else in the whole state of Kentucky."

"Thank ye kindly, Judge," the accused replied. "And I just want you to know that I couldn't have gived you one whit of trouble more than you've gived to me!"

The saddest indictment against mountain strip, or surface, coal mining that I've heard yet was delivered by a man at Lotts Creek in Perry County. He looked around at the once heavily forested mountains which had been denuded by stripping and sadly shook his head.

"It's gettin' so," he mused, "that a man can't hardly find a safe place around here no more to make whisky."

It doesn't have to do with moonshining, but since it still has to do with whisky making, let me tell you a story I heard in Anderson County.

A short prologue is needed to set the stage.

Although the work of government gaugers and checkers at distilleries now is done with professional and impersonal efficiency, that wasn't always the case. In fact, in less strict days it wasn't uncommon for the government men to sample the end product from time to time during their work day.

Years ago, before automobiles were too common, an old gent who lived in Lawrenceburg worked as a gauger at a distillery on the Kentucky River near Tyrone, some five miles away. He drove to and from work each day in a one-horse phaeton, an open buggy-like rig with rear wheels that were perhaps twice as large as the front wheels. It was his custom to nip along as the day progressed, and sometimes he'd be feeling no pain, as the saying goes, by the time he started home.

One day his fellow workers played a joke on him. They removed the wheels of his buggy, putting the larger wheels in front and the smaller ones on the rear of the rig. All the way home that afternoon he realized something was different, but he couldn't quite pin it down. Finally, as he pulled up at his house, it came to him.

"You know," he confided to a friend, "I've been making that round trip to Tyrone for 35 years, but this is the first time I ever realized that the drive back is uphill all the way!"

Down in Owensboro they tell about a temperance lecturer who appeared there in a series of meetings in the days before Prohibition. One night the speaker had gotten especially eloquent in describing the evils of strong drink — how it destroys the stomach, disrupts the digestive process, addles the mind.

In the middle of his speech, a man on the front row pulled a bottle of moonshine from his pocket and took a deep swig in full view of the audience.

"Brother, why did you do that?" the lecturer asked.

"Because you've said such awful things about what liquor will do to a man," came the reply, "I needed a drink to steady my nerves!"

Once after having been on a raid in Cumberland County, Big Six Henderson decided, on his way back home, to stop off at a remote crossroads store where, according to reports sifting into his office, moonshine was being peddled. Since he was dressed in clothes dirty and grimy from the raid, he had to do little more to disguise himself.

He thought. He rubbed some smudge on his face, poured a little of the whisky he'd seized on his shirt for aroma, and entered the store.

After passing the time of day with the keeper, he got down to business.

"I wonder where a man could get a good drink of moonshine around here," he asked in a low voice.

"My gosh, Bix Six," the store proprietor replied innocently, "if anybody knows, it ought to be you!"

The drinkers of merry St. Shear
See more than pink rats, folks fear.
Grey rabbits, blue bats,
And six-legged cats.
Leap out of their Budweiser beer.

WHOLESOME TOASTS
(To gladden the sober or otherwise — heart)
HERE'S to present day culture — which doesn't care about your English if your Scotch is all right.

Here's to love, the only fire against which there is no insurance.

Here's to the Chaperone,
May she learn from Cupid
Just enough blindness
To be sweetly stupid.

Here's to the doctor's prescriptions — fill 'em up again!

To woman in her higher, nobler aspects, whether wife,
widow, grass-widow, mother-in-law, hired girl, telegraph
operator, telephone helloer, queen, book agent, wet
nurse, step-mother, boss professional, fat woman, professional, double-headed woman and professional
beauty.
God bless her.

Mark Twain

Here's to the happiest hours of my life —
Spent in the arms of another man's wife:
My mother!

Here's head first, in a foaming glass!
Here's head first, to a lively lass!
Here's head first, for a bit of kissing,
For the good don't know the fun they're missing!

Here's to a temperance supper,
With water in glasses tall,
And coffee and tea to end with —
And me not there at all.

The good die young — Here's hoping that you may
live to a ripe old age.

Here's a toast for you and me:
And may we never disagree;
But, if we do, then to hell with you.
So here's to me!

CRISP TOASTS FOR FESTIVE NIGHTS

Drink to the girls and drink to their mothers,
Drink to their fathers and drink to their brothers;
Toast their dear healths as long as you're able,
And dream of their charms while you're under the
  table.

D. C.

Here's to woman! — ah, that we could fall into her
arms without falling into her hands!

Ambrose Bierce

Here's to our bachelors, created by God for the consolation of widows and the hope of maidens!

Let's be gay while we may
And seize love with laughter;
I'll be true as long as you
But not a moment after.

Here's to thee and thy folks from me and my folks;
And if thee and thy folks love me and my folks
As much as me and my folks love thee and thy folks
Then there never was folks since folks was folks
Love me and my folks as much as thee and thy folks.

"Here's to Woman — once our superior, now our
equal!"

Here are toasts to you. And you. And you.

Here's to the man who is wisest and best,
Here's to the man who with judgement is blest.
Here's to the man who's as smart as can be —
I mean the man who agrees with me.

Here's to matrimony — the high sea for which no compass has yet been invented.

Here's to the maid who is thrifty,
And knows it is folly to yearn,
And picks out a lover of fifty,
Because he has money to burn.

Here's to the girl who's bound to win
Her share at least of blisses,
Who knows enough not to go in
When it is raining kisses.

"Here's to Hell! May we have as good a time there as
we had getting there."

Here's to one and only one,
And may that one be he
Who loves but one and only one,
And may that one be me.

"Here's to the bride and mother-in-law,
Here's to the groom and father-in-law,
Here's to the sister and brother-in-law,
Here's to friends and friends-in-law,
May none of them need an attorney-at-law!"

A TOAST — A BENIGN STATEMENT!

Here's to the old-fashioned girl who used to stay home
when she had nothing to wear!

Here's to your car and my car — may they never
meet!

Here's to the liquor that makes a man see double and
feel single!

Here's looking at you — double.

Here's to the pedestrian; every year is leap year with
him!

We have toasted our sweethearts,
Our friends and our wives,
We have toasted each other
Wishing all merry lives;

Don't frown when I tell you
This toast beats all others
So drink one more toast, boys —
A toast to — "Our mothers."

Down with the reformers — their motto is "mirth control."

Ladies, ladies, why attack the only thing that improves with age.

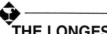

THE LONGEST BAR

In the days when drinking emporiums were known only as saloons many, if not all, Western states liked to claim a saloon "with the longest bar in the world ..."

We had one of those bars in the Northwest, and you should know that once upon a time the City of Portland, Oregon, was famed less for its gorgeous roses than for an institution commonly called Erickson's, a saloon patently designed for the refreshment of giants. It occupied the best part of a city block on Portland's Skidroad, which was, and is, Burnside Street, and its noble bar presented a total length of exactly 684 lineal feet. Men of Gath might have lifted their schooners here in comfort.

It was founded in the early eighties by August Erickson, an immigrant from Finland ...

Perhaps a score of Western cities staked claims to drinking places having "a mile-long bar." These turned out, I have discovered by no little research and occasionally by actual measurement, to have been bars of one hundred feet or less. Erickson's mighty total was no myth. It comprised five great bars that ran continuously around and across one gigantic room. Two of these ran from the Second Avenue side to Third Avenue. Two more connecting bars completed the vast quadrangle. And the other bar ran down the middle. Incidentally, the stretch of bar nearest the Second Avenue entrance was known, because Russians liked to congregate there, as the St. Petersburg.

Size alone probably would have brought fame to Erickson's, but the place offered much else. The bars, fixtures, and mirrors were the best money could buy. No tony twenty-five-cent place had better. There was a concert stage, on one side of which was "a $5,000 Grand Pipe Organ." Around the mezzanine were small booths where ladies were permitted, though no sirens of any sort were connected with the establishment. And no female was allowed on the hallowed main floor.

Art was not forgotten. Besides numerous elegant and allegedly classical nudes, there was a thumping great oil, "The Slave Market," which depicted an auction sale of Roman captives and was highly thought of by the connoisseurs of art who infested Erickson's. The late Edward (Spider) Johnson, onetime chief bouncer for Erickson, said it was common for these art lovers to weep into their schooners at the plight of the poor slaves.

Yet this was no place for tears. It was vital and throbbing with the surge of life, the place where men of the outdoors came to meet and to ease their tensions, a true club of working stiffs. Indeed, in time Erickson added an outside sign which designated his establishment as the Workingman's Club. Itinerants in funds made a beeline for the place. Five minutes after the swift *Telephone* or the graceful *Harvest Queen* docked, anywhere from fifty to five hundred wage slaves converged on Erickson's, like so many homing pigeons. Seven minutes after arrival of a Northern Pacific or a Southern Pacific train, in barged another crowd. It was said, and with some truth, that if you wanted to find a certain logger you went to Erickson's, and waited, he would be there soon or late. It was common, too, to address letters to footloose friends in care of Erickson's. The place often held hundreds of such missives waiting to be claimed.

Patrons of Erickson's discussed almost but not quite everything over their beverages. Jobs, wages, working conditions were popular subjects. Stupendous feats of work were bragged about; so, too, other foremen were praised or assassinated; but hot discussions of religion, economics, or politics were forbidden. The mildest form of discouragement from Erickson's corps of competent bouncers was a sharp word of admonition. This was followed, if not instantly heeded, by the bum's rush, performed by the finest practitioners procurable — of whom more later.

Men might forget the Erickson paintings, or even the
$5,000 Grand Pipe Organ, but no man ever forgot the
Erickson Free Lunch. This was really prodigious. On his
business cards August Erickson described this feature of
his place modestly as "A Dainty Lunch." The word was
not quite exact. Erickson's free lunch centered around
the roast quarter of a shorthorn steer, done to the right
pink turn that permitted juices to flow as it was sliced.
Bread for sandwiches was cut precisely one and one-
half inches thick. The Swedish hardtack bread, round
and almost as large and hard as grindstones, stood in
towering stacks. The mustard pots each held one quart.
The mustard was homemade on the spot; it would
remove the fur from any tongue. Round logs of sliced
sausages filled platters. So did immense hunks of
Scandinavian cheeses, including *gjetost* (of goat's milk)
and *gammelost* (meaning "old"), the latter of monstrous
strength; one whiff of it caused the weak to pale. "Gude
ripe," Gus Erickson said of it, and he did not lie. Pickled
herrings swam in big buckets of brine. At Christmas
generous kettles of *lutefisk* were added to the dainty
lunch.

Beer was five cents, and the local brew was served in
schooners of thick glass yet of honest capacity. I pos-
sess two of these veritable glasses. They each hold sixteen fluid ounces. Strong men used both hands to lift a
filled schooner. Genuine Dublin porter was a nickel a
small glass. Imported German brews cost a dime. All
hard liquor was two for a quarter. Lone drinkers were
looked askance, but when one did appear it was taken
for granted he would require not one but two glasses of
whisky.

The regiment of bartenders needed to operate a
saloon as large as Erickson's was carefully selected; the
men ran to grenadier size. All wore beautifully roached
hair. All had carefully tended mustaches. Across the
broad white vest of each was a heavy watch chain.

Below the vest was a spick-and-span apron. No coats were worn. There was no regulation in regard to neckties, but all bartenders' shirts were white. Arm elastics were an individual matter. Scandinavian bartenders liked pink; all others had a weakness for purple. Trousers were held in place by distinctly he-man galluses, the Hercules brand, fit to stand the strain of lifting a keg and the torsion incident to heaving a bung starter. The bartenders were known for their courtesy, and were able to converse learnedly about prizefighters, bike champions, and such; to give sound advice in matters of love or business; to prescribe suitable eye-openers, pick-me-ups, and for lost manhood.

All of the Erickson beverages were sound. A handsome likeness of August Erickson himself appeared on the label of the house whisky. He was a good looking, even a studious-appearing man, blue-eyed, blond, and had a neatly curled mustache. He wore, oddly enough for one of his occupations, pince-nez with gold chain. His broadcloth suits were tailored for him. He was a man who liked order, and this applied to his saloon.

Order in Gus Erickson's was kept, with rare recourse to the city police, by his own staff. My friend, the aforementioned Spider Johnson, was for a period chief of these bouncers. Spider was a tall, genial, and most courteous man, and of many intellectual interests. He handled men well, too. But when stern necessity called, he was lightning-quick, and carried a punch that was rightly feared. One of his staff was a delightful person known as Jumbo Reilly. He was big, well over three hundred pounds, and though he really wasn't much of a fighter, his size and general aspect were so forbidding that he had no difficulty holding his job. "Jumbo," Spider recalled, "had the appearance of a gigantic and ill-natured orangutan. He also could emit a hideous laugh-snarl that cowed almost any one except the most stout-hearted. His fighting tactics were to fall boldly upon his opponent. While not fatal, this was very discouraging. Jumbo's special ability lay in his version of the bum's rush. It was swift and expert."

A favorite story around Erickson's, which had five entrances from three streets, concerned a character called Halfpint Halverson, a troublesome Swede logger who liked to argue about the comparative abilities of different nationalities. On one such occasion, when he disregarded Jumbo Reilly's warning, the bouncer plucked Halverson by the collar and pants and threw him out the Second Avenue entrance. Halverson presently wandered in through one of the three Burnside Street doors. Out he went again in a heap. This continued until he had been ejected through four different doors. Working his way around to the Third Avenue side, Halverson made his entry through the fifth door. Just inside stood the mountainous Jumbo. Halverson stopped short. "Yesus" he said, "vas yu bouncer en every place dis town?"

Loggers loved places as big as that.

Gus Erickson was a man who took things as they came. His place was but two short blocks from the waterfront, and when what is still referred to as the Flood of Ninety-Four made much of downtown Portland something like Venice, and his own and most other saloons were inundated. Gus promptly chartered a big houseboat, stocked it complete, including the Dainty Lunch, and moored the craft plumb in the center of Burnside Street. Men in rowboats, homemade rafts, catamarans, and single loggers riding big fir logs came paddling for succor to Erickson's floating saloon. Spider Johnson remembered that a score of customers never once left the place during the several days of flood.

The glory of Erickson's lasted for nearly forty years. Prohibition did not close it, nor did it become a bootlegging establishment. It simply carried on halfheartedly with near beer and added an out-and-out lunch counter, not free.

The paintings of the pretty plump nudes, and even "The Slave Market," were sold. So was the $5,000 Grand Pipe Organ. The size of the place was cut in half. The bar when I first saw it ran to no more than two hundred feet, and this has been reduced again, to fit the new and dreary times. August Erickson himself died in 1925, in mid-Prohibition. Repeal did not bring a return to the great days; Oregon's liquor law permits the sale of beer over a bar, but not whisky.

Thus does Erickson's, still the Workingman's Club, survive as a shadow of its former immensity. The stuffed head of a deer, sad-eyed and disconsolate, is all that remains of the stupendous old wall *décor.*

*Beer, tea, milk, and — God forbid — soda pop are the only beverages to pass over the mahogany. Yet the fame of Erickson's has not wholly evaporated. Every little while some old-timer, filled with nostalgia, stops off in Portland for no other reason than that of seeing if the longest bar in the world still retains its old-time polish. It does, but there is less than sixty feet of it left. Perhaps this is just as well, for within a block of the old saloon is now a manicure parlor that caters to lumberjacks and other now thoroughly tamed men. In such a civilization, there could be no place for the lusty joint that was Erickson's.

*Reprint from *Far Corner*, by Stewart H. Holbrook with permission from his daughter Sibyl Holbrook.

Some merry old monks in Manila,
Found life was growing much dulla,
So they brewed a great ale,
In a homungous tin pail,
And they and their lives were much fulla.

Walkin' whiskey vat: A heavy drinker.

GENE PERRET'S FUNNY BUSINESS:
Part Five: *Executives Perks & Peeves*

There was one guy at work whom nobody knew was a drunk. But one day he came to work sober ... after that they knew!

The executive at an important conference passed out. But they brought him to. Then they brought him two more and he was able to continue.

George Emmick had a unique, very special recipe for his meal at his favorite cafe. It began: "Squeeze the juice from one bottle of gin ..."

Bob Hope loved to tell this joke about when he played golf with Dean Martin. "I sure do like to play golf with old Dino. If he wins, we tell him."

The boss invited two of his junior executives to lunch. He wanted to learn a bit more about them and they, of course, were anxious to impress the boss. The chief thought he'd test their intellectual level and asked, "Do you gentlemen care for Omar Khayam?"

One youngster said, "I do, in moderation. But I much prefer Zinfandel. And that was that until the two young guys got back to the office. "You dumb cluck," the one guy said. "If you don't know what Omar Khayam is, don't fake it ... just say so!"

"Yeah? Well, what in hell did I say?"

"Never mind! Zinfandel isn't a wine, jerk, it's brandy."

Gene Perret's Funny Business by Gene and Linda Perret. ©1990. Reprinted with permission of Prentice Hall, Englewood, NJ.

"YOU SEEM LIKE SUCH A MARVELOUS, INTERESTING CONSIDERATE, INTELLIGENT PERSON. WHAT OTHER IMITATIONS DO YOU DO?"

Drunks sober up. Fools remain fools.

Jack and Jill went up the hill,
But not for a drink of water ...
And that's why they both fell down,
They drank what they hadn't oughta.

Jim Jones was a confirmed drunk, but nobody knew it. Then, one day, he was shaving and cut himself so badly his eyes cleared up and THEN everybody knew!

A junior executive got so upset at the boss that he had a big lunch and several martinis with it. When he got in his car, he picked up the president of the company who had "tee'd" him off and called up the guy on his car phone. He made the connection and called him all the foul names in the book. "Further," he went on, "I'm sorry I ever worked for your goddam Company!"

"Man do you know, whom you are talking to? This is the President of the company!"

The irritiated executive said, "Well, do you know who you are talking to, Mr. President?"

"No, I don't!"

"Good," said the caller and hung up.

An office party has been described as a place where you can say, "I'm gonna tell my goddam boss exactly what I think of him, if it's the last thing I do!" And, generally, it is!

Two pints make one quartet.

The master of poetic fiction, Dylan Thomas, told this story on himself — of his stupidity at a party. He was very drunk and talking freely on and on. Then, suddenly, he stopped. "Somebody is most boring around here and, dammit, I think it's me!"

You can be sure you talked too much, said too much at the office party if, upon driving to work the next day, you see your office desk in a truck going the other way! Then, when you get to your parking place for work, you see that it has been sealed off with a one inch rope! That should do it for you.

At lunch one day, an executive was heard to say: "I just can't make up my mind what kind of food to order for lunch. I've eliminated all but the olive or the twist."

Then there was the typical executive's luncheon order: "I'll have my usual lunch today, waiter. Hold the food!"

The two-martini lunch is wonderfully good for a certain type of salesman ... he sells swizzle sticks!

There is one particular restaurant in my town that simply does not serve alcohol. It's true that they don't serve many executives, either.

Whiskey: A good servant but a rotten master.

William Penn, our early American statesman, was a Quaker.

On this day, he was advising a young drunkard on how to rid himself of his drinking habit.

"But it's as easy as opening thy hand," said Penn.

"Explain what you mean and I'll do it," said the drunk.

"When thee has a glass of liquor in thy hand, simply open thy hand before it reaches thy mouth and thee will never drink again."

Leaden-headed with a hangover, W. C. Fields was asked if he'd like a Bromo Seltzer. "Hell no," he replied, "I couldn't stand the noise."

A guy, real tight after four cocktails, runs to catch the ferry that normally takes him home. As he staggers up to the gangplank, he sees the ferry about twelve feet from shore. He backs up, then weaves and runs and jumps on board ship to collapse on the deck. "Hey, I-I-I m-made it!" he chuckles.

"Yeah," said a member of the crew, "If you'd only waited! We were pulling up to the shore!"

The bar is really crowded, every seat is taken. A huge, terribly fat woman walks in, glares around her, then shouts: "Ain't any of you gents gonna offer me a seat?"

A guy at the middle of the bar stands and says, "Lady, I'm sure willing to make a contribution."

One rule is certain: Don't try to keep both your business and yourself in a liquid condition.

A bar is raucous with laughter when a newcomer asks the bartender why everyone laughs when somebody calls out a number. Just then, a guy yells "twenty-two" and the place dissolves in laughter.

Suddenly, a guy calls out "sixty-two!" But nobody laughs.

"How come?" the new man asks. "I thought they laughed when a number is called?"

"You know how it is," the bartender replied, "some guys just can't tell a joke."

A drunk wandering down the street, stops a pedestrian and asks, "Shir ... c-could you t-tell me where I am?"

"You're on the corner of 57th Street and Fifth Avenue."

"Hell, man, I don't need d-details. Jusht tell me what c-city I'm in!"

———————

"I always keep a supply of stimulant handy in case I see a snake. I always keep a supply of snakes handy, too."

W. C. Fields

———————

Water kills more people than booze ... remember The Flood?

———————

Johnny O'Brien was a remarkable drinker ... he was the only one known who could light the candles on a birthday cake by blowing on them.

———————

Three guys started arguing, getting louder and louder until the bartender said, "If you guys don't quit your noisy argument in here, well ... why don't you do your arguing and fighting outside! Come back in when you quit your fighting!"

Soon they came back in and the bartender asked, "So? What happened?"

One of the arguers said, "I couldn't believe it! Those guys pulled out razors!"

"Holy smokes! What happened?"

"Nothin'. There wasn't no place to plug 'em in!"

———————

A guy sitting at the bar seems so depressed, the bartender asks if he can do anything to help him.

"Y'see," the guy replies, "I got a 210 I.Q. and can't find a soul to talk with."

"I can help," the bartender said and introduces him to an intelligent regular customer and they began to discuss the philosophy of Kant, the music of Wagner and nuclear physics.

The bartender sees another loner, equally depressed, goes over to him and asks, "You, too, seem depressed. Can I help?"

"Well," the guy says, "I got an I.Q. of 115 and nobody to talk to, pal around with."

"Hey, I'll fix that!" says the bartender. "Come with me!" He walks over to George and introduces the two guys. They hit it right off, talking about baseball, Forrest Gump and income tax rates being way too high.

The bartender goes to a third guy. "What's buggin' you, buddy?" he asks.

"Me? My I.Q. is only 83 and I ain't got nobody to talk to."

"Hey, you've got to meet that fellar sittin' at the end of the bar. He's your man."

The two low I.Q. guys sit down together and one says to the other: "How's your re-election campaign movin' along?"

It is a truism among drinkers that cocktails and women's breasts have much in common. For example, one isn't enough and three is too many.

A guy buys drinks for everyone in the bar and, finally, hands the bartender a bottle cap to pay the bill.

"Whataya think you're doin'?" The bartender screams.

"Don't worry. Just keep track of the bottle caps and I'll pay you before I go home."

When ready to leave, many drinks later, the guy goes to the bartender and says, "I'm leavin'. How many bottle caps?"

"There are fifty-eight caps in all."

"Good," replied the cap-happy customer. "Got change for a manhole cover?"

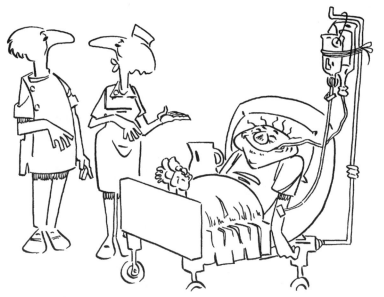

He has a bottle hidden somewhere in here.

LAST CHAPTER

As we come to the conclusion of this bit of fun, let's take a look at an article telling us about drinking in the sixteenth and seventeenth centuries, when our nation was part of the British Empire. The scene: a tavern in colonial America in what was then the social center of the colonies ... the tavern.

SWIPSY OR SOBER?

The supervisor of drinking does his duty, 17th and 18th century.

"Mingle me a flip Landlord," the guest ordered.

The tavern-keeper glanced doubtfully toward the stout, red-faced man in brown homespun. Already he had drunk enough to be rated as blue, perhaps even damp. And he seemed bent on drinking right down the list posted beside the bar.

"Alicante ... Calibogus ... Constantia ... Ebulum ... Flip." He had successfully reached the F's, but there was trouble ahead. "Kill-devil ... Metheglin ... Mumbo ... Rumbullion." He might well manage metheglin, a strong, sweet drink made of fermented honey and herbs, which was mead, the draught of the Druids and Vikings. But kill-devil and rumbullion were straight Barbadoes and New England rums, branded by reformers as "hot and hellish liquors" but beloved by imbibers as banishers of care woes and ills. Kill-devil, they declared, really did kill devils or at least knocked them unconscious until next morning. On top of the foundation already laid, straight rums might stagger even a seasoned toper. And the end of the list was not yet.

"Switchell ... Spiced Syder ... Stonewall." Surely if the guest survived to order them his sibilants at least would be slipping, and the effect of the last-listed, a potent mixture of hard cider and rum, would resemble a head-on collision with the structure for which it was named.*

"A flip and make haste." The second demand was louder and more importunate.

The red-faced man was a traveler, a stranger. Consequently his name was not upon another list affixed to the wall behind the bar, a roster of known drunkards to whom the sale of liquor was strictly forbidden. Reluctantly acknowledging the order, the tavern-keeper nodded to his tapster. From a shelf containing an imposing array of tankards, beakers, punch bowls, flagons, posset-cups, jugs and mugs, the tapster took down a four-quart flip glass. He filled it two-thirds full of strong beer, sweetened it with molasses and several pinches of dried pumpkin. Then he poured in a generous gill of rum and set the concoction down before the drinker.

*Alicante and Constantia were sweet red wines from Spain and Africa respectively; calibogus — cold rum and beer; ebulum — eldeberry wine; mumbo (short for mumbo-jumbo) — rum punch; switchell — a mixer of molasses, water, vinegar, and rum.

That worthy rose and strode a bit unsteadily toward the great open fireplace. Its warm glow turned his rubicund countenance redder still. Deep within it burned a back-log, so large it had been necessary to drag it in by a chain hitched to a horse. On the hearth various dishes were cooking, filling the taproom with savory odors. In a long-handled skillet a bear steak sizzled. A roast of beef, a large wild turkey which must have weighed close to fifty pounds, and a haunch of venison revolved, browning, on a spit. It was turned by the mechanism of a treadmill on which a small, leashed dog walked endlessly, his mouth watering as the meat juices dripped in the pan beneath the spit. They would be sopped up by diners with hunks of rye-and-injun — bread made from rye flour and corn meal. In a brass kettle, swung from the crane, simmered a soup or a pudding.

No attention to the contents of pots, pans, and kettles and the alluring spectacle presented by the skewered roasts was paid by the flip drinker, a grave error on his part. The hard and steady drinking, so prevalent throughout the American Colonies, usually was accompanied — and its effects mitigated — by as hearty and simultaneous eating, especially of meat.

The rubicund gentleman, however, was concentrating on assuaging a thirst. He bent over the hearth and from a bed of coals drew the short, small poker called a loggerhead or flip-iron or flip-dog. Whistling and holding it like a torch, he carried it back to his table and plunged it, hissing, into his creaming glass of flip. He grasped the great glass in both hands and drained it, smacking his lips over the scorched, puckering taste which made flip a favorite drink of the day.

"Ahhh!" he sighed gustily. A beatific but somewhat vacuous grin wreathed his face. He might now fairly be described as slightly fuddled. A few more and he would be decidedly haily gaily. Others of the company, watching him, glanced apprehensively around the taproom.

"Tapster," roared the red-faced one, peering over at the list of drinks, "bring me a mug of kill-devil and tarry not."

"No more!" a stern voice decreed.

The drinker swung around on his bench to glare up at the lank and lugubrious individual who had suddenly appeared at his elbow. An uncomfortable silence was broken by the red-faced man's bellow: "And who might you be, Master Nosey, to interfere with my pleasure?"

"I am the Supervisor of Drinking," the owner of the commanding voice identified himself. "It is my duty to visit the inns and ordinaries of this town and prevent drinking to excess. If I lay eyes on any man who has ordered a drink too many — more than he can soberly bear away — I am empowered by ordinance to countermand it."

All the company in the taproom nodded in mournful confirmation. Strict regulations and restrictions on excessive drinking had been in force in most of the Colonies since the middle of the Seventeenth Century. Taverners were fined or lost licenses if any frequenters were found "disguised with drink" on their premises; even if they allowed a guest to tipple more than half an hour or to drink after 9 o'clock in the evening, or consume more than a limited amount at other than meal time. As liquor became more plentiful and cheaper — in Boston in 1686 the Reverend Increase Mather had declared that the poor and wicked could make themselves drunk for a penny — punishments multiplied in number and variety. Drunkards were disenfranchised and forbade holding office. They were fined, flogged and put in work gangs. In 1638 in Virginia two married couples were chastised for intoxication by being confined in stocks during church service. As an erring sister might be sentenced to wearing a scarlet "A," so might a bibulous brother be ordered to "weare about his necke, and so to hang upon his outward garment a D made of red cloth and set upon white; to continyu this for a yeare, and not to have it off any time he comes among company." New Yorkers, caught in their cups, were forced to drink three quarts of salted water laced with lamp oil. Yet always the aim of the authorities was to restrict drunkenness, not drinking.

"Very well, Master Kill-joy, you have the power," the red-faced one ungraciously conceded. "But how do you know when to exercise it? How do you determine I've had one too many as you maintain?"

"By my own good judgment," the Supervisor affirmed.

The other sniffed. "So you presume to settle a moot question that has been agitated for centuries. Sages have vainly attempted to settle whether a man be swipsy or sober. Who are *you* to say?"

"I have had no little practice hereabouts," the Supervisor affirmed. There was a shuffling of boots, and a series of rueful grins ran around the taproom. "And," he continued, "I am informed as to the various statutes and tests applied in this and other Colonies. Both Maryland and Virginia define a drunkard as one who has been intoxicated thrice."

"You have no knowledge of how oft I've been fuddled, Master Nosey."

"None, Master Jorum," the Supervisor admitted, giving him the name of a drinking-bowl. "But when I behold the number of drinks you have encompassed, I will hazard that the occasions have not been seldom. Now Maryland specifies that drunkenness is: 'Drinking to excess to the notable perturbation of any organ of sense or motion.' You might try repeating that though I doubt you are able. My own favorite test is this: 'When the same pair of legs which carried a man into a house cannot bring him out it is a sufficient sign of drunkenness.'"

"But my duty, sir," he continued, "is to nip it in the bud — to prevent anyone becoming bereaved or disabled in the use of his understanding. And I shall never be a popular man," he finished sadly.

"Bah!" Red-face exclaimed. "You are but a bigot. I doubt not that you drink only water or at best small beer."

"You shall see!" The Supervisor was justly indignant at so monstrous an accusation. "Tapster, a flip."

The drink was quickly placed before him. He plunged a hot loggerhead in it and drank. Supervisor and Red-face resumed their argument. It became more heated. Shaking flip-irons in each other's face, they were, as the saying went, "at loggerheads."

Gleefully the company in the taproom hunched forward over their tables. They came to the tavern not only for meat, drink, and warmth and because they were lonely but for relief from boredom. In the tavern (the equivalent of the community center of much later days) were held court sessions, musters, elections, and entertainments — showings of wax-works and freaks, performances by ventriloquists and trained animals, dances, concerts, lotteries. Scarcely second to these, was a good, rousing argument like the one now developing. Everybody sat back to enjoy it.

The Supervisor still held the floor. "Tests to determine when the limits of sobriety are passed were established by the Bishop of London himself," he declaimed. "It is highly regrettable that they had to be devised for the clergy of Virginia, given to roistering. His Grace decreed that any clergyman might be proven to be drunk simply if he stayed an hour or longer in the company where they were imbibing ardent spirits and in the meantime drinking healths or otherwise taking his cups as they came 'round."

"Had I a drink before me," interposed Red-face, "I would propose a health. It might even be yours."

The Supervisor ignored him. He continued: "The Bishop also made mention of such signs that a minister was swipsy as: Striking, threatening to fight, or laying aside any of his garments for that purpose. Also staggering, reeling, vomiting, or incoherent, impertinent, obscene or rude talk."

"Amen for the Bishop," the other rudely interrupted. "Far more revealing are the stages of intoxication as described by a good Parson Weems in his pamphlet entitled, *The Drunkard's Looking-Glass*. They should assist your endeavors greatly, Master Nosey. Let me name them for you." He ticked off on his fingers. "Stage One — a Drop in the Eye. Two — Half-sleeved. Three — a Little on the Staggers. Four — Capsized. Five — Snug under the Table with the Dogs. Six — Able to Stick to the Floor without Holding on."

A roar of appreciation echoed through the taproom. Everybody ordered another drink, including the Supervisor. Somebody slipped one to the deeply grateful red-faced man. It went unnoticed by his argumentative opponent who was bursting with a retort.

"All very diverting," he caustically observed. "Mirth, like wine, maketh glad the heart of man, as the Psalmist declares. But we are discussing a serious question. Far more useful than the Weems whimsies is this enumeration of the symptoms of drunkenness by the celebrated Doctor Benjamin Rush of Philadelphia." He drew a broadside from his pocket and began to read, glancing up after each item at Red-face.

"'First symptom: unusual garrulity,'" he read. "'Second, unusual silence.' No one could convict you on that score, Master Jorum. 'Third: captiousness and a disposition to quarrel.' Now there I have you."

Everybody laughed, Red-face louder than the rest, and everybody ordered another drink. With extra relish the Supervisor read the next items:

"'Succeeding symptoms: uncommon good humor, and an insipid simpering or laughing. Profane swearing and cursing. A disclosure of their own or other people's secrets. A rude disposition to tell persons what they

know of their faults. Certain immodest actions —
particularly by women.'"

Somebody called for three hearty cheers for the last-
mentioned symptom. They were given with a will.
Everybody had another drink. The Supervisor read on
with greater gusto:

"'Ninth: a clipping of words. Tenth: fighting. Eleventh:
singing.'"

The company seized the occasion to raise a jolly
drinking song until the rafters rang. When it ended, the
Supervisor and the Red-faced one were clapping each
other on the back. The latter scanned the broadside
lying on the table and exclaimed:

"Shay, ol' friend, here's shymptom you forgot to read.

"'Shympton Number Twelve: imitating noishes of brute
animals.'"

"Aye," the Supervisor acclaimed. "Bes' shymtom of
'em all. *Woof, woof!*"

A CHANTY OF DEPARTED SPIRITS
by Christopher Morley

The earth is grown puny and pallid,
   The earth is grown gouty and gray,
For whisky no longer is valid
   And wine has been voted away —
As for beer, we no longer will swill it
   In riotous rollicking spree:
The little hot dogs in the skillet
   Will have to be swallowed with tea.

O ales that were creamy like lather!
   O beers that were foamy like suds!
O fizz that I love like a father —
   O fie on the drinks that are duds!
I sat by the doors that were slated
   And the stuff had a surf like the sea —
No vintage was anywhere vatted
   Too strong for ventripotent me.

I wallowed in waves that were tidal,
   But yet I was never unmoored;
And after the twentieth seidel
   My syllables still were assured:
I never was forced to cut cable
   And drift upon perilous shores,
To get home I was perfectly able,
   Erect, or at least on all fours.

Although I was often some swiller,
   I never was fuddled or blowsed:
My hand was still firm on the tiller

No matter how deep I caroused;
But now they have put an embargo
   On jazz juice that tingles the spine,
We can't even cozen a cargo
   Of harmless old gooseberry wine!

But no legislation can daunt us:
   The drinks that we knew never die:
Their spirits will come back to haunt us
   And whimper and hover near by.
The spookists insist that communion
   Exists with the souls that we lose
And so we may count on reunion
   With all that's immortal of Booze.

"Shay, offisher, wheresh th' corner?"
"You're standing on it."
"'S no wonder I couldn't find it!"

CATAWBA WINE
by Henry Wadsworth Longfellow

This song of mine
Is a song of the vine,
To be sung by the glowing embers
Of wayside inns,
When the rain begins
To darken the drear Novembers.

BREATHES THERE THE MAN
by John Mistletoe

Breathes there the man with soul so dead
Who never to himself hath said
Last night I drank the fizz too deep,
Last night the fizz was fountainous!
Whose heart hath ne'er within him burned,
   Whose brain ne'er waggled.
As home his footsteps he hath turned
   And danced or straggled
Feeling the pavement sway and leap —
   Last night the streets were mountainous!

If such there breathe, go mark him well!
For him no bacchic raptures swell;
High though his titles, proud his name,
Aquarian bliss let fishes claim!
Despite his titles or position,
The wretch, the friend of prohibition,
Living, shall forfeit harmless laughter,
Dying, shall merit no hereafter,
Parched in the dust from whence he slunk,
Unwept, untoasted, and undrunk!

Spectator — "Hey! Sit down in front!"
Drunk — "Don' be ridiclish. I don' bend that way."

DRINKING
by Abraham Cowley

The thirsty earth soaks up the rain,
And drinks, and gapes for drink again.
The plants suck in the earth, and are
With constant drinking fresh and fair;
The sea itself — which one would think
Should have but little need of drink —
Drinks ten thousand rivers up,
So filled that they o'erflow the cup.
The busy sun — and one would guess
By's drunken fiery face no less —
Drinks up the sea, and when he's done,
The moon and stars drink the sun:
They drink and dance by their own light,
They drink and revel all the night.
Nothing in nature's sober found,
But an eternal health goes round.
Fill up the bowl, then, fill it high,
Fill up the glasses there; for why
Should every creature drink but I;
Why, man of morals, tell me why?

HERMIT HOAR, IN SOLEMN CELL
by Samuel Johnson

"Hermit hoar, in solemn cell,
Wearing out life's evening gray,
Smite thy bosom, sage, and tell,
What is bliss, and which the way?"

Thus I spoke; and speaking sigh'd,
Scarce repressed the starting tear;
When the smiling sage replied —
"Come, my lad, and drink some beer."

AND YOU MAY RECALL THIS
by Don Marquis

"I wanchya meeta 'nol' 'nol' frien' o' mine!"
"Umgladdameetcha! Bill's frien's my frien's, too!"
"Thish frien' besh frien'! I gotto open wine!"
"You gotto le'me buy thish drink f'r you!"
"I gotto buy thish drink f'r 'nol' 'nol' frien'!"
"Now, lishen, Jim! You gonna love thish lad!"
"Billsh friensh is my friensh to th' bitter en'!"
"Now, lishen, Jim! thish besh frien' ever had!"

Honest, hardworking drunkards! Hour by hour
They toiled on at their chosen task until
They bent beneath the burdens that they bore,
They bent and swayed, sustained but by the power,
Each one, of his indomitable will,
Which ever bade him conquer just one more.

This drunk sways his way into his house at two in the morning. His wife comes downstairs, takes one look and says, "Swine!" He looks up, smiles and says, "No, dearie, 'swhiskey."

When Eve, upon the first of men
The apple pressed with spacious cant,
Oh, what a thousand pities, then,
That Adam was not Adamant!

Thomas Flood

For sure ... two pints make one cavort.

Two men waited their turn at the crowded green on the golf course. While they waited, one of the two pulled from his golf bag a bottle of whiskey and offered it to the other fellow.

It so happened that the guy who was proffered the drink was not only a teetotaler but detested drinks and drinkers, saying: "I'd just as soon go to a hog house, scoop up a shovel-load of manure and eat the lot as to take a drink of your whiskey!"

The drinker thought a moment, then said: "Well, I suppose it all depends on what a feller gets used to!"

There was an old Fellow of Trinity,
A Doctor well versed in Divinity,
But he took to free thinking
And then to deep drinking,
And so had to leave the vicinity.

Arthur Clement Hilton — 1851-1877

THE MORNING AFTER

A Gilded mirror, a polished bar,
A million glasses, straws in a jar:
A courteous young man, all dressed in white
Are my recollections of last night!

The streets were dirty and far too long,
Gutters sloppy and policemen strong:

The slamming of doors in a sea-going hack;
That's my recollection of getting back!

The stairs were narrow and hard to climb,
I rested often for I'd lots of time:
An awkward keyhole, a misplaced chair,
Told the folks plainly I was there!

A heated interior, a wobbley bed,
A sea-sick man with an aching head:
Whiskey, beer, gin, booze galore,
Were introduced to the cuspidor!

And with morning came bags of ice
So very necessary in this life of vice;
And when I cooled my throbbing brain,
Did I swear off and quit? No, I got soused again.

My Pious Friends and Drinking Companions
Frank Shay and John Held, Jr.
N.Y.: The Macauley Co., 1928

CHANTEY OF NOTORIOUS BIBBERS
I

Homer was a vinous Greek who loved the flowing
    bottle,
Herodotus was a thirsty cuss, and so was Aristotle.

Chorus

Sing ho! that archipelago where mighty Attic thinkers
Invoked the grape to keep in shape, and lampooned
    water drinkers.

II

King Richard fought the heathen Turk, along with his
    Crusaders,
On wabbly legs they tippled kegs and hated
    lemonaders.

Chorus

Sing ho! the gallant English King; sing ho! his merry
  yeomen
Who felt the need of potent mead to make them
  better bowmen.

III

Bill Shakespeare loved to dip his pen in Mermaid Inn
  canary,
And Bobby B. was boiled when he indited "Highland
  Mary."

Chorus

Sing ho! the buxom barmaid Muse who did her work
  on brandy,
She now eschews such vulgar brews and trains on
  sugar candy.

IV

Dan Webster stoked his boilers with brown jugs of
  apple cider,
And when he made a speech he yanked the spigot
  open wider.

Chorus

Sing ho! those spirited debates, bereft of all
  restrictions,
When statesmen carried on their hip the strength of
  their convictions.

Innocent Merriment, An Anthology of Light Verse,
by Franklin P. Adams, Garden City Publishing Co. New York: 1945.

THIRD CAVALRY SONG

Oh, I belong to the — hic! — Third Cavalry, —
   Hic! And a little bit more!
In my back yard I've got a — hic! A distillery, —
   Hic! And a little bit more!
In my front yard I've got a brewery and a wine press
   If they go wrong I'm in a hell of a fess.
For I belong to the — hic! — Third Cavalry, —
   Hic! And a little bit more.

R-E-M-O-R-S-E

PADDY MURPHY

The night that Paddy Murphy died
I never shall forget!
The whole damn town got stinking drunk
And they're not sober yet.

There is one thing they did that night
That filled me full of fear:
They took the ice right off the corpse
And stuck it in the beer.

That's how they showed their respect for
   Paddy Murphy,
That's how they showed their honor and
   their fight,
That's how they showed their respect for
   Paddy Murphy
They drank his health in ice-cold beer that night!

QUARTERMASTER SONG

[*Refrain*]: My eyes are dim, I cannot see;
I have not brought my specs with me;
I ... have ... not ... brought my specs with me.

For it's whisky, whisky, whisky,
That makes you feel so frisky,
   in the corps, in the corps.
For it's whisky, whisky, whisky
That makes you feel so frisky
   in the Quartermaster Corps.

For it's gin, gin, gin,
That makes you want to sin,
   in the corps, in the corps.
For it's gin, gin, gin
That makes you want to sin
   in the Quartermaster Corps.

For it's beer, beer, beer,
That makes you in*sin*cere,
   in the corps, in the corps.
For it's beer, beer, beer
That makes you in*sin*cere
   in the Quartermaster Corps.

For it's scotch, scotch, scotch,
That gets you in the crotch,
   in the corps, in the corps.
For it's scotch, scotch, scotch

That gets you in the crotch
   in the Quartermaster Corps.

For it's ale, ale, ale,
That gets you by the tail,
   In the corps, in the corps.
For it's ale, ale, ale
That gets you by the tail
   in the Quartermaster Corps.

For it's rye, rye, rye,
Puts tears into your eye,
   In the corps, in the corps.
For its rye, rye, rye
Puts tears into your eye
   in the Quartermaster Corps.

[*Refrain*]: My eyes are dim, I cannot see;
I have not brought my specs with me;
I ... have ... not ... brought my specs with me.

Reprinted from *Rowdy Rhymes*
White Plains, N.Y.: Peter Pauper Press, 202 Mamavo-WCU Ave.

WHISKEY JOHNNY
(an old, old chant sung by sailors)

Whiskey is the life of man, Whiskey, Johnny!
Oh, I'll drink whiskey while I can, Whiskey for my
   Johnny!

Oh whiskey straight and whiskey strong,
Give me some whiskey and I'll sing you a song.

O whiskey makes me wear old clo'es,
Whiskey gave me a broken nose.

Whiskey killed my poor old dad,
Whiskey druv my mother mad.

If whiskey comes too near my nose,
I tip it up and down she goes.

I had a girl, her name was Lize,
She puts whiskey in her pies.

My wife and I can not agree;
She puts whiskey in her tea.

Here comes the cook with the whiskey can,
A glass of grog for every man.

A glass of grog for every man,
And a bottle full for the shantyman.

Song of American Sailormen by Joanna Colcord
New York: W. W. Norton and Co., Inc. 1935

Whiskey: It kills germs, but how can you get them to drink it?

American Slang About Drinks, Drinkers and Drinking

The word, BOOZE didn't come to the American language until the mid-1800s. LIQUOR came earlier, in the 1700s. "STRONG WATER" was the preferred term used by our colonial forefathers.

But RUM was an early word. A shortened version of RUMBUSTION or RUMBULLION. In fact, RUM was used to indicate all liquors, not just the specific drink. Early on, Rum was called STINK-A-BUS.

BOURBON did not enter common usage until the 1850's. Earlier it was called CORN WHISKEY. Later, in the late 1870's, it was called MOONSHINE. Irving Cobb, superb American humorist (1876-1944), said: "When you absorb a deep swig of it, you have all the sensation of having swallowed a lighted kerosene lamp!"

The places that sell us our wingding materials had and have amusing names, most of them apt if uncomplimentary. Here are a few:

barrel house	gargle factory	layout
booze joint	exchange	pothouse
boozery	fill mill	rat hole
bottleshop	gin dive	rum hole
cocktail lounge	gin mill	rum/gin/or whiskey joint
crib	grog shop	shebang
doggery	hell hole	spot
dramship	hole	waterhole
drinking booth	honky-tonk	whiskey hole
drinkery	hooch house	watering hole
dump	joint	watering place
firetrap	juice-joint	whiskeymill

The generic term for liquor had funny, imaginative and quite descriptive slang terms. Below...some of them.

anti-freeze	firewater	nut	smile
anti-lunch	flash flip	old man's milk	snifter
appetizer	forenoon	panther piss	snort
aqua aguardiente	forty rod	peg	something damp
bald-face	gargle	phlegm cutter	soother
barley dew	gill	pick-me-up	soul-destroyer
base-maker	glug-guzzle	pill	stingo
belt	grapple-the-rail	pine top	stone fence
blue ruin	gutwarmer	pistol shot	strong water
bottle earthquake	hard stuff	poison	strychine
brave-maker	heel tap	prairie dew	swig
breaky leg	hell broth	railroad	swizzle
bucket bumper	honeydew	red ink	tad
bug juice	hooch	red disturbance	tanglefoot
bumblebee	Indian whiskey	red-eye	tangler
bun clink	infernal compound	refresher	tarantula
bust skull	invigorator	reposer	tarantula juice
caper juice	Jersey lightning	reviver	taste
chic	jiffer	riser	tequila
coffin nail	jig juice	rotgut	the real thing
coffin varnish	johnny	rowser	thimbleful

conversation fluid	jolt	sauce	tift
corn	kill-the-beggar	scamper juice	timothy
cowboy cocktail	lightning	scorpion bible	tipple
dehorn	liquid fire	screech	tiswin
delight	lush	settler	tongue
deoch-n-doras	mescal	shant sparkler	tonsil varnish
digester	modicum	sheep-dip	toothful
drinkwater	moonshine	sheepherders' delight	tornado juice
dust cutter	morning rouser	shifter	trade whiskey
dynamite	mountain dew	shot	valley tan
educated thirst	neck oil	simon-pure	whiskey
eye-opener	night cap	ski	white mule
fancysmile	nip	slug	white wash
finger	nose paint	slut	wild mare's milk

The very act of drinking liquor has many synonyms, and here are a few:

to beer	a digester	a warmer
to bend	an eye-opener	a willy-watcher
to blink	a fancy smile	liquor-up
to booze	a flip	to look thru a glass
to bub	a go	to moisten the lips
to budge	a hair of the dog	to mop-up
to crush a bottle or	that bit me	to potate
glass or cup	a heel tap	to prime oneself
to crook the elbow	an irrigator	to drive another
(or the little finger)	a leaf of the old author	nail in ones' coffin
to damp your mug	a morning rouse	to revive
to dip one's nose	a modicum	to rock
to drown the rose	a nip	to save a life
to fuddle	a nightcap	to shed a tear
to flush	bit of medicine	to shout
to gargle	pistol shot	to slosh
to guzzle	a pony	to sluice the ivories
to go see one's paw	a pill	to splice the mainbrace
to take an ante-lunch	a quencher	to suck the monkey
a little anti-substance	a refresher	to swill
an appetizer	a revelation	to swig
a bead	a rouse	to swizzle

a bait of tape
a bosom friend
a bumper
a chit-chat
a cheer
a corker
a cooler
some corn juice
something damp
a damper
a drain

a repose
a smile
a swig
a sleeve-button
a shout
a snooter
a sparkler
a settler
a soother
a thimble ful
a tift
a toothful

to take the pin out
to take a drop in the eye
to take in some O-be-joyful
to tiff
to tipple
to toddy
to wet one's whistle
to wine

There are many phrases common to inviting another to have a drink. Here are a few:

About time for a smile, isn't it?
Come and see your pa.
How'll you have it?
How about a tod?
How about driving another nail?
How about a suck of corn juice?
Laddie boy, your utmost.
Let's go and see the baby.
Let's liquor up.
Let's get there.
Let's drive another nail.
Let's stimulate.

Name your medicine.
Nominate your pizen.
Try a little anti-abstinence.
Wet your whistle.
What'll you have?
What's your medicine?
Will you take a nip?
Will you try a smile?
Will you irrigate?
Will you tod?
Your whiskey's waiting.

And here are some slang phrases indicating acceptance of the above offers:

Accepted without a doubt.
Anything to oblige.
Count me in.
Don't care if I do.
Here's at you.
Here's how.
Here's into your face.

None too soon either.
On time.
Sir, your most.
Well, I don't mind.
Well, I will.
With *you*, yes.
Yes sir..reee.

I accept and unconditionally
subscribe and then some.
I'm thar.
I'm with you.
Laddie boy, your utmost.

Yes sir! Put her there.
Yo dang betcha.
You bet and yes siree!
You do me proud.

Whiskey is the common drink of many Americans and here
are a few lovely synonyms you can use in asking for it:

aqua vitae
bald-face
barley bree
bottle-earthquake
brave-maker
breaky leg
bug juice
bum-clink
caper-juice
curse of Scotland
family-disturbance
farintosh
forty-rod lightning
gargle

grapple-the-rails
grog
hard stuff
hell-broth
infernal compound
kill-the-beggar
lightning
liquid fir
mare's milk
moonlight
mountain dew
neck oil
old man's milk
pine-top

railroad
red-eye
rotgut
screech
simon pure
sit-on-a-rock (rye whiskey)
soul-destroyer
square-face
stone-fence
tangle-foot
the real thing
the sma' still
white-eye

Gin, too, has a great number of slang words replacing its
three letters. The next time you want a drink of gin, ask the
bartender for:

blue ruin
blue-tape
cat-water
cream of the valley
daffy
diddle
drain
duke

eye-water
frog's wine
jackey
juniper
lap
max
misery
old Tom

ribbon
satin
soothing-syrup
stark-naked
strip-me-naked
tape
white satin

Beer is the drink of choice for most Americans. And it, too, has a great many synonyms. Here are a few:

Act of Congress	bunker	perkin
American burgundy	cold-blood	ponge
artesion	gatter	rosin
barley	half-and-haf	rot-gut
belch	heavy-wet	sherbert
belly-vengeance	hevy	stingo
brownstone	John Barleycorn	swankey
bum-clink	knock-me-down	swipes
bung-juice	oil of barley	swizzle

Similes to describe just how drunk a person is are legion. Here are a few to be used as needed:

blind drunk	drunk as a brewer's fart
crying drunk	drunk as Bacchus
dead drunk	drunker'n blazes
drunk as a Cleveland fiddler	drunk as a fiddler
drunk as the devil	pissing drunk
drunk as a fly	so drunk he couldn't see a hole
drunk so as to barely hang together	through a ladder
drunk as hell	so drunk he had to open his
drunk as a lord	collar to piss
drunk as boiled oil	tumbling drunk
drunk as a tapster	

To go on a spree, a real beerfest or drink blast, here are a few words to describe just what it is:

bat	hellbender	stew
bender	hooley	tear
boose-up	jag	toot
branigan	randan	twister
bust	rip	whooper-dooper
caper	shindy	wingding
guzzle	soak	

And a simple drink of your favorite stuff can be named and ordered in a number of ways. Of course, the important thing is that you get it! And any of these words stand a good chance of succeeding.

Hey, bartender, slip me a shot, ball, bump, bumper, drag, finger, gargle, geezer, gluz, guzzle, hook, hooker, jigger, jolt, kick, nip, peg, pull shot, slug, slurp, snifter, spot, suck, swallow, swig, tot, toot.

Now for some words to describe the act of drinking: Bend the elbow, Booze, Chug-a-lug, Crook the elbow, Down a few, Fight the bottle, Gargle, Hang a few on, Have a dram, Have a gargle, Have a nip, Hit the booze, Hit the bottle, Hit the sauce, juice up, Knock back, Knock off, Lap up, Liquor up, Slug down, Slurp, Souce, Splice the main brace, Swig, Swill, Tank, Tank up, Tip the elbow, Toss off, Wet one's goozle, Wet one's whistle.

For sheer numbers, units of American slang, the synonyms for drunk top them all. One estimate puts the number of slang words for drunkenness at 667! It takes a lot of years and a lot of drinks to develope that much slang. Here are a few of them, English words used to describe one who is "under the influence," or, put plainly ... DRUNK! With these in hand, no one should be at a loss to describe a drunk!

activated (very drunk)	bloated	bottled
alkied	blotto	boxed
annihilated	blowed away	bunned
aped	blue	buzzed
awawsh	boiled	buzzy
bagged	bombed	caged
basted	boozed	canned
behind the cork	boozed up	canned up
blind drunk	boozy	clinched
blitzed out	boracho	clobbered

cockeyed
comboozelated
cooked
corked
corned
crashed
crocked
cross-eyed
cronk
crumped out
dead drunk
dead to the world
decks awash
discombobulated
discouraged
dipsy
drunk as a boiled owl
drunk as a coot
drunk as a fiddler's bitch
drunk as a lord
drunk as a skunk
edged
electrified
elevated
embalmed
faced
faint
far gone
feeling good
feeling no pain
feshnusked
flaked out
flooey
floozified
flying high
fractured

fried
fried to the gills
fizzled
gassed
ginned
ginned up
glassy-eyed
glazed
gone
gonged
googly-eyed
had one too many
half-bagged
half-corned
half-crocked
half in the bag
half-lit
half-screwed
half seas over
half-shaved
half-shot
half-slewed
half-snaped
half-sprunk
half-stewed
half under
happy
having a buzz on
having a load on
having an edge on
having a skinful
having a snootful
having a snoot full
having one too many
high
high as a kite

hooched up
illuminated
impaired
in a bad way
in color
in one's cups
in the bag
in orbit
in the ozone
juiced up
jungled
kited
knocked out
laid out
lathered
liquified
liquored
liquored up
lit
lit up
lit up like a Christmas Tree
loaded
looped
looping
lubricated
lushed
lushed up
muggy nupped
maggoty
mashed
muddled
non-compos pooped
obfuscated
oiled
on the shikker
organized

ossified
overserved
overtaken
pafisticated
petrified
pickled
pie-eyed
[Brit] pifflicated
pissed
plonked
plotzed
polluted
poopied
potted
pubbled
reeling
ripe
ripped
riproaring
drunk
roaring drunk
rocky
rummed up
saturated
sauced
schnockered
screwy
scronched
seeing pink elephants
shaved
shellacked

shikker
shitfaced
shot
slewed
sloshed
slugged
smashed
snozzled
snoozamarooed
snuffy
soaked
soupy
soused
sozzled
spiffed
spifflicated
sprung
squiffed
squiffy
squiffy-eyed
stewed
stewed to the gills
stiff
stinking
stinking drunk
stinko
stitched
stoned
swacked
swacko
swizzled

swozzled
tangle-footed
tangle-legged
tanked
tanked up
tanky
three sheets to the wind
tight as a tick
toasted
topsy-boozy
tuned
under the infuence
under the table
up to the ears
up to the eyeballs
up to the gills
up a tree
upholstered
varnished
vegged out
waxed
wiped
wiped out
woozy
zapped
zagged
zissified
zonked
zonked out
zonkers

The End

BIBLIOGRAPHY

Brick Lining, Brick Smith. *The Sun Sentinel,* Ft. Lauderdale, FL

Cartoons by Martin J. Bucella, Cheektowaga, NY

Cartoons by Jack Corbett, Salem, OR

Cartoons by Benita Epstein, Cardiff-By-The-Sea, CA

Cartoons by Oliver Gaspirtz, Brooklyn, NY

Cartoons by Walt Hendrickson, Rockford, IL

Cartoons by Tom Jackson, Pacifica, CA

Cartoons by Masters Agency, Capitola, CA

Cartoons by Luci Meighan, Laytonville, CA

Cartoons by Eldon Pletcher, Slidell, LA

Cartoons by Dan Rosandich, Chassell, MI

Cartoons by George Wagner, Highland Hts., KY

Cartoons by M. L. Zanco, Waukegan, IL

Esar's Comic Dictionary, by Evan Esar. Amereon, Ltd., NY

Far Corner, Stewart Holbrook.

Gene Perret's Funny Business, by Gene & Linda Perret. 1990. Prentice Hall Publishers. Englewood, NJ

Grandma's Little Books, Dorothy Galyean,
Springdate, UT

Hometown Humor, U.S.A., Loyal Jones and Billy Edd
Wheeler. 1991. August House, Little Rock, AR

Horsing Around, Lawrence Clayton and Kenneth W.
Davis, Editors. Wayne State University Press,
Detroit, MI

Innocent Merriment, Franklin P. Adams. 1945.
Garden City Publishers, New York, NY

***I Always Tell the Truth (Even If I Have To Lie To Do
It),*** Chris Morley. 1990. The Greenfield Review Press,
Greenfield Center, NY

Joe Creasons Kentucky, Joe Creason. Brown-
Forman Corp., Louisville, KY

Men Only, John Henry Johnson, Editor. 1936.
Maxwell Droke, Publisher, Indianapolis, IN

My Pious Friends and Drunken Companions, Frank
Shay. 1930. The Macauley Company.

Noah S. Sweat, Jr. article from Political Classics,
Corinth, MS

Our Lusty Forefathers, Fairfax Downey. 1947. John
Hawkins & Associates, Inc., NY

Pecos Tales, 1967. Texas Folklore Society,
Nacogdoches, TX

Pun American Newsletter, Deerfield, IL

Rowdy Rhymes, 1952. Peter Pauper Press, Inc., White Plains, NY

Savvy Sayin's, Ken Alstad. Ken Alstad Co., Tuscon, AZ

Songs of the Cowboys, compiled by N. Howard Thorp, University of Nebraska Press, Lincoln, NE

Stiff as a Poker, Vance Randolph. 1993. Barnes & Noble Publishers, New York.

The Booze Book — Joy of Drink, Ray Russell. 1965. Playboy Press, Chicago, IL

The Old Time Saloon, George Ade. 1931. Richard R. Smith, Inc., NY

The Wolfpen Notebooks, 1991. University Press of Kentucky, Lexington, KY

Treasury of American Anecdotes, B. A. Botkin. 1982. Galahad Publishers, NY

Also available from Lincoln-Herndon Press:

*Grandpa's Rib-Ticklers and Knee-Slappers	$ 8.95
*Josh Billings — America's Phunniest Phellow	$ 7.95
Davy Crockett — Legendary Frontier Hero	$ 7.95
Cowboy Life on the Sidetrack	$ 7.95
A Treasury of Science Jokes	$ 9.95
The Great American Liar — Tall Tales	$ 9.95
The Cowboy Humor of A. H. Lewis	$ 9.95
The Fat Mascot — 22 Funny Baseball Stories and More	$ 7.95
A Treasury of Farm and Ranch Humor	$10.95
Mr. Dooley — We Need Him Now! The Irish-American Humorist	$ 8.95
A Treasury of Military Humor	$10.95
Here's Charlie Weaver, Mamma and Mt. Idy	$ 9.95
A Treasury of Hunting and Fishing Humor	$10.95
A Treasury of Senior Humor	$10.95
A Treasury of Medical Humor	$10.95
A Treasury of Husband and Wife Humor	$10.95
A Treasury of Religious Humor	$10.95
A Treasury of Farm Women's Humor	$12.95
A Treasury of Office Humor	$10.95
A Treasury of Cocktail Humor	$10.95

*Available in hardback

The humor in these books will delight you, brighten your conversation, make your life more fun, and healthier, because "Laughter is the Best Medicine."

Order From:

Lincoln-Herndon Press, Inc.
818 South Dirksen Parkway
Springfield, IL 62703